DIAMONDS FOR PROFIT

DIAMONDS FOR PROFIT

Fred Cuellar

Diamond Information Line: 713-22-CARAT
Internet Web site: http://www.diamondcuttersintl.com

Photograph of Fred Cuellar by Gittings Lorfing
Cover and inside photography by Leeming Studios • 401-941-9459
Media Relations & Marketing: LaTeace Towns-Cuellar

DEDICATION

This book is dedicated first to my mother and father. This book would not be possible without their love and support.

Second, I dedicate this book to top diamond expert Rick Antona. Without his calculations on the "dumping" tables this book would not have been possible.

Third, and most of all, I dedicate this book to the love of my life, La Teace. She makes life worth living and I could not imagine a better companion with whom to spend all the days of my life.

Special Dedications

To John and Anthony. Thanks for the inspiration.

To "Silky," my personal assistant. You make everyday sunny by your presence. Thanks for taking care of me.

To Nick, my friend, my editor, my alter ego. You take my words and make them soar.

CONTENTS

LIST OF ILLUSTRATIONS

LIST OF TABLES

THE PREMISE

Buy low, sell high. Any questions? You want me to elaborate? Oh, okay. Let's start by noting that each year over six *billion* dollars worth of new diamonds are sold in the United States. That's a lot of diamonds. Multiply that by, say, the past twenty years. That's a *helluva* lot of diamonds. Where do all those diamonds go? On rings and bracelets and necklaces and tiaras and brooches and earrings and studs and watches and tie tacks and *objets d'art* and Lord only knows what else.

It would be nice to think that all of these precious stones find happy homes and stay there, to be handed down through the generations. Nice, but not true. The truth is, more than half of all marriages fail. That makes for a lot of homeless engagement rings. A lot of people die every year, or go broke, or bankrupt. That's a lot of jewelry for the heirs, the auction block or the pawn shop. *Diamonds are forever—but diamond owners aren't.* The point is, over $3.0 billion worth of diamonds are *resold* each year in the secondary market. And here's the juicy part: 95% of them are sold for ten cents on the dollar!

Think of it: *Ten cents on the dollar.* A wise man said, "A penny saved is a penny earned." Let me coin a phrase for the diamond trade: "A diamond bought at the right price is a fortune earned." The key, of course, is the *right price*. The purpose of this book is to help you determine that magical "right price." *You can make money buying and selling diamonds. This book will reveal how to do it.*

We'll take the trip to profitability in three steps:

1. **The Treasure Hunt**—How to *find* the diamonds.

2. **The Sherlock Holmes**—Deducing the value of the diamonds. It's elementary!

3. **"Doing the Donald"**—Making the deal. (Named in honor of Donald Trump, the man who seems to be able to make something from nothing!)

In my experience, I've found that there are three basic types of people who buy and sell diamonds. These are the One-Timers, the Part-Timers, and the Major Leaguers. I've divided this book into three parts—three separate books, really, to help you make money from diamonds at whatever level you operate.

One-Timers are people who have diamonds to sell, for one reason or another, and want to realize a bit of quick cash from the sale. Perhaps a marriage has failed and you want to get rid of the rings, or perhaps old Aunt Nellie (God rest her soul) has left you a diamond brooch and you'd rather have the cash. You'll take your diamonds into the secondary market, sell them, and be done with it. This book will help you get the most cash for your diamonds in the least amount of time.

Part-Timers are those folks who both buy and sell diamonds for a little adventure, or for a side line or hobby to bring in extra income. Part-Timers always have their antennae out, looking for opportunities to make some cash. They don't want to give up their day job, but they enjoy the challenge of making money on the side buying and selling diamonds. This requires a little more work—and we'll go into more detail—but the financial rewards can be substantial. The skills you'll learn from this book will help you to seize opportunities and cash in on them.

Major Leaguers are making a career of trading in diamonds. These are the people who are willing to put in a lot of time, a lot of work, and accumulate a lot of knowledge. It's not easy—but the financial reward can be practically unlimited. If you work hard, and diligently apply the lessons you learn here, you can make thousands or tens of thousands a month! But before you rush down to the Mercedes dealer and order your new wheels, you've got to put in the time and the effort that this level of diamond dealing requires. And don't skip! If you're heading for a new career, get comfortable with sections I and II before moving on.

TALKING THE TALK

Every line of work has its own language. You probably talk to your co-workers in a language that outsiders would find a bit strange. We all use trade jargon and technical terms—the little verbal secret handshakes that identify us as insiders. The jewelry industry is no different, and I'm going to teach you the lingo to make you sound like an insider. You know that when you take your car to a mechanic, the less you sound like you know what's going on under the hood, the bigger the dollar signs that dance in the mechanic's head. It's the same story when you deal with jewelers and appraisers and others in the jewelry industry. If you talk the talk, they're less likely to try to take advantage of you. So here's the lingo. Remember the definitions, and put these terms to work for you:

Retail Whew! What the heck *does* this word mean anymore? It used to mean the price that the end user—the consumer—paid for merchandise. But *nobody* pays retail anymore! It's become a pejorative term, as in, "Did you see Betty's new Mercedes? I heard she paid retail for it!" Translation: Betty's a fool.

How much of a markup is a "retail" price? 20%? 50%? 100%? 400%? Answer: All of the above. It's easier to think of retail in these simple terms: **Retail is the highest price you can pay for merchandise.**

Wholesale Just like the term "retail" (and the Old Gray Mare), this "ain't what it used to be." "Wholesale" used to be the price of goods or services before marking them up for the consumer. But now there are wholesale clubs, places where the consumer pays the so-called wholesale price. Let's give wholesale a simple definition: **Wholesale is the best price you can pay for merchandise.**

Don't confuse wholesale with dealer cost. "Dealer cost" is what the dealer pays the manufacturer for merchandise, plus his[1] overhead. He will mark up the goods in order to make a profit when he sells them. Dealers, also called vendors, are very competitive, always trying to undercut each other's prices. But nowadays they sometimes find themselves in competition not only with other vendors, but also with their own suppliers, the manufacturers. Many manufacturers have found it more profitable to sell directly to the consumer. This drives the vendors nuts, and in some cases drives them right

---

[1] By the way, I almost always refer to jewelers and appraisers and others in the diamond industry as *men*. No sexism intended here—just a convenient shorthand. There are many women in the business, and they can be as good, and as bad, as the men.

out of business, because competing with the manufacturer is a battle the retailer can't win.

Let's refine the definition of wholesale and say that **the wholesale price is a less-than-20% markup over the dealer's cost.**

Example 1: Tony the Fish Dealer buys fish off the boat, adds in his overhead and determines his "dealer's cost" to be $1.00 per pound, and sells it to you for $1.10 per pound. Is he selling at (a) retail or (b) wholesale? *Ding, ding, ding*—you are correct; he's selling at *wholesale*, because Tony's markup is only 10%, and any markup under 20% is wholesale.

Example 2: Sam the Fish Man buys fresh fish from the fisherman on the dock, adds in his overhead and determines his "dealer's cost" to be $2.00 a pound. He sells it to you for $1.00 a pound. Is Sam a (a) wholesaler, (b) retailer, or (c) idiot? Hah! Just wanted to see if you were paying attention. Seriously, if Sam's "dealer's cost" is $1.00 per pound and sells it to you for $2.00, he's selling at *retail*, because his markup is more than 20%.

Forgive me for belaboring this point, but it's fundamental to the lessons in this book, and if we don't understand wholesale and retail, we'll never understand "dump value" or the other concepts we need to know to buy and sell diamonds.

TIME OUT!

I've tried to make this book as easy as possible to understand, but I know that sometimes you'll have questions. So I've set up a help line staffed by very competent people. Feel free to call with your questions. The help line is open Monday through Friday from 9 A.M. to 6 P.M. (Central), and Saturday 9 A.M. to noon. Who knows, I might answer it myself!

Diamonds for Profit Help Line: (713) 222-2728

Okay, on with our Lingo Lesson:

Rapaport   We know that retail is paying too much, and wholesale is the right price. In the diamond trade,

Rapaport = Wholesale

Rapaport is a wholesale price guide for diamonds. It lists specific prices for all shapes, grades, colors, and sizes up to six carats. Because diamond prices are constantly fluctuating, the Rapaport guide is published weekly by the Rapaport Diamond Report at 15 West 47th Street, New York, NY 10036.

- If I say I'm selling or buying a diamond at "Rap value," this means that I'm selling/buying at wholesale.

- If I say I'm selling or buying at "Rap plus 10," this means that I'm possibly selling/buying the diamond at 10% over wholesale, or paying wholesale plus a premium for a better proportioned diamond.

Dump Value   This is a biggie! If you don't understand dump value, you won't make a dime with diamonds. Here's what it means: **Dump value is the diamond's immediate cash liquidity value.**

Speak English, Fred! Okay, looking at it another way, dump value is the rock-bottom price of a diamond, the lowest possible price, *the price a dealer will most likely offer you for your diamond*. There's a formula for determining dump value: **Dump value = 60% of Rapaport for fair or well-proportioned diamonds.**

That means dump value is 60% of wholesale, since Rapaport = Wholesale. Let's say a diamond has a wholesale value of $10,000, as determined by the Rapaport guide. Its dump value is 60% × 10,000, or $6,000. Don't ever forget, dump value is 60% of *wholesale*, not 60% of *retail*. Since retail could be any markup over wholesale, 60% of retail will cost us money. Remember, our goal is to buy low!

Buying low and selling high
Never, never makes us cry.

Selling low and buying high,
Kiss your hard-earned bucks goodbye.

Let's say you're thinking of buying a diamond and reselling it to make some moolah. You take the diamond to an appraiser, who says it's worth $8,000. Here's another fact of life to remember: **Appraised Value = Retail.**

So, if an appraiser is going to give you a retail value, why bother with the appraiser? Because the appraiser will also give you the Rapaport value if you ask, and will give you the information you need to find the Rapaport value on your own—the weight, color, clarity, and cut of the diamond. On the Rapaport sheet you find the diamond's *wholesale* value is $4,000. Therefore, the dump value is 60% × $4,000 or $2,400. **You must be able to determine the dump value of any diamond you want to buy or sell, or you may wind up paying too much for it or selling it for too little!**

Example: Your grandmother leaves you her diamond wedding set, and your sister says, "Oh, I'll buy it from you for $2,000." How do you know if she's offering a fair price? You take the rings to an appraiser and find that the Rapaport value of the set is $5,000. You take 60% of that and find that the dump value is $3,000. So you gently tell your sister to take a hike—or hike her offer to at least $3,000. **Never accept less than dump value for your diamonds!**

Example: A friend at work broke off his engagement, got his ring back, and wants to sell it. He tells you he had the ring appraised for $10,000, but he'll let you have it for $3,300. Sounds good, but before you reach for your checkbook, ask him if you can take the ring to an independent appraiser. He agrees, and your appraiser tells you the Rapaport value of the ring is $4,000. We take 60% of that, and arrive at a dump value of $2,400. Your friend's asking price is $900 higher than the dump price, and unless he lowers his price to $2,400 you pass up the deal. **Never pay more than dump value for diamonds you're trying to make money on!**

Of course, the worth of anything is what someone else is willing to pay for it—someone else may come along and give the guy whatever he's asking, simply because the buyer *likes* the ring and doesn't care that much about the price. But when you're in the business to make money, you can't let emotions affect your decision. One day I was admiring a painting a friend had bought. He told me he paid $50,000 for it. To him, it was a thing of beauty, a joy forever, and worth the price. To me, it was just a few bucks' worth of paint in a $200 frame. As beautiful as some jewelry is, we must learn to look at it for its cash value, its liquidity value. That's the only way you'll be successful buying and selling diamonds for a profit. If buying and selling for a profit is not your goal, you should be reading my first book, *How to Buy a Diamond*. It exclusively deals with the primary market and collectors whose primary concern is not the bottom line.

So, to repeat, dump value is the highest price you should ever pay for a diamond, and the lowest price you should ever sell a diamond for. Let's move on.

The Four C's   Four factors determine the value of a diamond: *Color, Cut, Clarity,* and *Carat Weight.* Let's take a look at them, one at a time.

Carat Weight refers to the actual weight of the diamond. One carat is one-fifth of a gram, or 200 milligrams. The word *carat* is derived from *carob*, and in ancient times in the Mediterranean region, the carob bean was used to measure the weight of a diamond—one bean equaled one carat. In the Far East, four grains of rice were used to equal one carob bean, or one carat. Some old-timers in the diamond business still refer to a one-carat diamond as a *four-grainer.*

Clarity is determined by how free the diamond is from *blemishes* and *inclusions.* Blemishes are surface flaws such as scratches, nicks, and chips. Inclusions are internal flaws such as carbon, cracks, and crystals. If you can't see the flaws with your naked eye, the diamond is said to be *eye clean*. Diamonds that are eye clean have the highest resale value, so let's rule out any diamonds that are not eye clean from our business. If you can see blemishes or inclusions with your eyes, the diamond is a commercial-grade stone, not eye clean, and is to be avoided. Remember, diamonds are valuable because of their rarity, their beauty, and their durability. Commercial-grade diamonds are not rare and not too beautiful, so leave them alone.

Color doesn't refer to the colors that radiate from the diamond when it sparkles, but to the overall body color of the diamond. Most diamonds are white, but diamonds occur naturally in other colors—red, blue, green, bright yellow—which are called "fancy" colors, rare and expensive. For our purposes, let's stick to white diamonds. The rule is, the whiter the better. The more yellow a diamond is, the less it's worth, unless it's a bright yellow (canary), which is a fancy color. Look at a diamond on a pure white background under good light to get an idea of its color grade.

Cut refers to the shape of the diamond and to how well-proportioned the diamond is. The proportions are very important to the sparkle of the diamond, and a poorly cut stone won't sparkle nearly as much as one that's cut well. Most diamonds are cut poorly, unfortunately, and this robs them of their sparkle. Here are the most common diamond shapes.

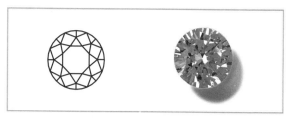

Round

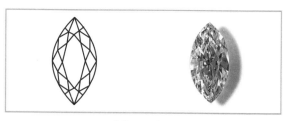

Marquise

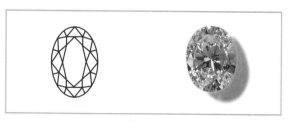

Oval

Pear

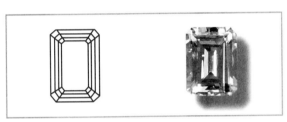

Emerald Cut

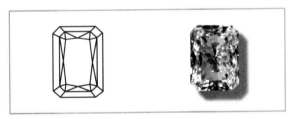

Standard Radiant

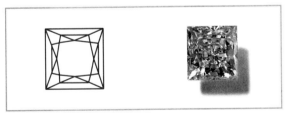

Princess

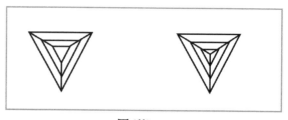

Trilliant

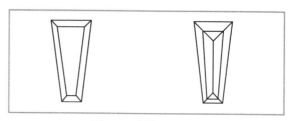

Tapered Baguette

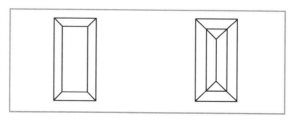

Nontapered Baguette

Okay, we've laid a foundation of basic diamond knowledge. In the next section we'll see how to put this knowledge to work.

Story Time

In my many years in the jewelry business, a lot has happened to me. Most of it has been good, some of it has been great, and some of it has been wonderful beyond my fondest dreams. But there have also been days when I "shoulda stayed in bed," days when I got caught napping and made bonehead mistakes that cost me a lot of money. Throughout the book I'll share with you some of these "stories of sweet success" and "tales of woe." I'm sure you'll make your own mistakes, but if I can teach you to avoid repeating *my* mistakes, I've already saved you thousands of dollars!

SECTION I
THE ONE-TIMER

THE TREASURE HUNT

At some time in your life, you will own jewelry. I feel pretty confident making that statement, because since time immemorial human beings, rich and poor, in virtually every culture in the world, have prized and collected precious metals and gems. It must be a rare person indeed who goes through life without ever possessing a piece of jewelry. And the fact that you're reading this book tells me you probably do own some jewelry. It might be an engagement ring or a wedding set that you purchased yourself. Perhaps it's something you received as a gift, or it might be jewelry you inherited. The fact that you're reading this book also tells me you're interested in converting that jewelry into cash or trying to figure out how to get or own diamonds cheaper than through the normal avenues like mall jewelry stores or JC Penney.

What we're going to talk about in this chapter is where to find these baubles, bangles, and beads, and how to convert your jewelry collection into a collection of portraits of great Americans—such as Ben Franklin's portrait on the $100 bill, if that is your final goal.

The Family Jewels

Inherited jewelry is a windfall—it doesn't cost you anything, and quite often it's something you don't wear anyway. Now, I know that some inherited jewelry carries great sentimental value. For example, you wouldn't give up your mother's engagement ring at gunpoint, because it was handed down from *her* mother, and the stone had been won in a poker game by great-grandpa Sam, and Mom gave it to you to place on the finger of the woman you love—you get the idea. But you might also be holding a diamond pin that came to you through the estate of the late and unlamented Aunt Biddie, who whacked you with her ivory-handled cane for stepping in her delphinium bed during your one and only visit to her plantation when you were seven. It's the pieces like this that you're willing and eager to convert into currency, and when you do, it's pure profit. Where do you find the family jewels?

A. Safe Deposit Box—How long since you inventoried your safe deposit box? Think hard. You may have jewelry in there that you haven't seen, much less worn, for years. You put it there because (1) it was valuable, and (2) you didn't want to wear it. Go get it!

Then think about other family members who might be holding something in *their* safe deposit boxes for you. Maybe you inherited some jewelry when you were a minor and your mother, father, or Uncle Jeremy tucked it away in their safe deposit box and forgot about it. Check with them, and if they have something of yours, ask 'em to fork it over.

B. Jewelry Box—You'd be amazed at the number of people who have completely forgotten what's in their own jewelry box or

4

chest. You wear something for a while, then you get something new, and the old piece goes into the box and gets submerged under a layer of costume jewelry and forgotten. Empty the entire contents of your jewelry box onto a clean, white sheet and do an inventory. You may be surprised at what you find. And be objective about this: If you find something you don't wear anymore, put it on the "For Sale" pile.

C. Fingers, Ears, Wrists, and Neck—That's right: the stuff you wear every day. Make a cool appraisal of each piece, asking yourself, "Would I rather have this ring, or this bracelet, or would I rather have the cash to buy something else?" Add it to the "For Sale" pile. In your mind, separate the stones from the setting. If there's a mounting you really like, then think about having the diamonds pulled out for sale and putting some less expensive stones in the mounting.

D. Family and Friends—No, I'm not telling you to become a jewel thief, or even asking you to go door-to-door begging for baubles. I *am* telling you that your family members and close friends may have some jewelry *they* would like converted into cash, and would be happy to let you do it for them and give you a piece of the action. Lots of people have old jewelry sitting around gathering dust, and they let it sit there because they don't even think about it. And when they do think about it, they haven't the foggiest idea how to sell it (sort of like you before you read this book). Make a list of family and friends, and then go to them and play "Let's Make a Deal." Tell them you're planning to get *your* old jewelry appraised so that you can sell it, and if they have anything they'd like to sell, you'll handle the transaction for a small fee. Don't accept less than

10% of the selling price—it wouldn't be worth your while—and if they'll accept a 50-50 split, so much the better!

E. The Boulevard of Broken Dreams—Only you know where this place is, but the tangible reminders of a busted engagement or a failed marriage could be anywhere. I'm talking about the engagement rings and the wedding sets. Where did *they* go when the romance went south? You might have been so hurt and angry that you tossed them into the deepest lake you could find, and some day you'll read a story about a retired mail clerk who hauled a six-pound bass out of that lake and *found a one-carat diamond ring in the fish's stomach!* Then you'll *really* be hurt and angry. But chances are you didn't heave the rings overboard. Instead, you tossed them into a sock drawer or a flower vase or some other place where you wouldn't have to see them. Think hard, and go find them, because I'll tell you this: *Diamond engagement rings are the single most valuable article of jewelry you can sell.* If you're the one who bought the rings in the first place, you probably paid full retail, and the thought of getting wholesale for them makes you sick.

Don't let this stop you from selling the rings. I'll give you two good reasons why. First, wherever it's been hiding, the ring has not been earning interest. Get the most money you can for it—this book will tell you how to do that—and put that money to work for you. Second, *you may be able to get your full purchase price back, even if the jeweler's return period has expired!* How? I'll tell you how.

It's a fact that the Federal Trade Commission requires that when a jeweler sells a diamond, it must be within *one grade* of its stated clarity and color, and within *one-half point* of its stated weight (one carat = 100 points). If it isn't, that's misrepresentation, and you're entitled by law to a full refund.

It's also a fact that the average jeweler *does* misrepresent the diamonds he sells, by an average of *two* grades in color and clarity, and as many as *ten points* by weight.

Of course, you have to find in your files the original appraisal the jeweler gave you when you bought the ring. With that in hand, have the diamond independently appraised. If it falls outside the FTC guidelines, you are entitled to get your money back no matter how long you've owned the diamond. *Getting* the money is a little more difficult, though. Read on.

The independent appraisal proves that your jeweler misrepresented the grades and weight of the diamond. Appraisal in hand, you march into the store and demand your refund. The jeweler gives the diamond the once-over and immediately goes into his "jeweler's denial mode." He tells you that it's not the same diamond he sold you, he's never seen this diamond in his life, and would you please get out of his store. What can you do? Not much, actually. It's what you *should have done,* rather than march in with his original appraisal and your new, independent appraisal.

What you should do is to walk in and say, "Hi there. I'd like a new appraisal of this diamond I bought from you five years ago." Show the jeweler the ring and his original appraisal, but keep your independent appraisal out of sight. The jeweler will then appraise the ring at exactly what he did originally, only adjusting the dollar value for inflation. *Then* you pull out the independent appraisal and say, "Aha! You agree that this is the same diamond I bought from you five years ago. But I've had it independently appraised, and it's not the quality and weight you said it was. I want my money back!" Threaten to go to the media and picket his store. Chances are you'll get your money back.

Even if the jeweler's original appraisal was accurate, you may get a full store credit toward a new piece of jewelry, and you'll be able to get rid of the old unwanted engagement ring and at least come out even.

Okay, we've completed our Treasure Hunt. We've gone through our jewelry boxes, safe deposit boxes, and other storage places. We've gotten jewelry from family members and friends to sell on commission. We've even retrieved the old engagement ring or wedding set from the bottom of the well. Now we're ready for the next steps: evaluation and appraisal.

The Gift
A Story of Sweet Success

One day a few years ago, I boarded a jetliner in Houston, bound for New York. When I had stowed my carry-on bag and buckled myself in, I looked over to see who I had for a seat mate. I saw a small, elderly lady, sitting straight and prim in her seat, clutching her handbag and trying very hard not to appear concerned. I guessed this lady had not flown often in her life. I leaned over and reminded her gently that she would have to stow her handbag before takeoff.

"Oh, thank you," she said. "I'm a little nervous, to be quite frank. I've never flown before."

I asked her why she was traveling to New York.

"Well," she said with a sigh, "I'm going to live with my daughter. She's meeting me at the airport. You see, my husband of fifty-five years passed away recently and my daughter doesn't want me living alone."

I offered condolences and, trying to brighten her up, I said she was lucky to have enjoyed such a long marriage.

"Thank you. Yes, I was fortunate. We had a good marriage, and now it seems like the time went by so fast . . . seems like just yesterday we were saying our vows." She was quiet for a long moment, replaying some cherished moments of her married life, before she returned to our conversation.

"And what about you?" she asked. "Why are *you* going to New York?"

I told her I was in the diamond business and was going there to close a deal on some diamonds.

"Oooh, diamonds!" Her lined face brightened. "Charlie—that was my husband—always said I'd have a diamond one day. When we got married, all we could afford were the wedding bands. Then came the children, and with one thing or another we never did have enough money for luxuries. Every anniversary Charlie would say, 'My dear, next year we'll get you that diamond!' But now there is no next year."

She bowed her head and tried not to let me see the tears, but eventually she had to dab them away with a handkerchief tugged from the pocket of her old coat.

In that moment, this sweet woman's tears revealed to me why I was on that plane, sitting beside her. I asked her name.

"Evelyn," she told me. "Evelyn Benson."

"Well, Evelyn," I said, "my name is Fred Cuellar, and I just realized that fate has brought us together. What is your ring size?"

"I—I don't know, really," she stammered. "Why?"

"Because I am here to give you your diamond ring. Charlie had something to do with seating us together, I'm sure of it." I guessed her ring size at about a six, and I had a grin sized extra large at this point.

"But I can't afford it," she protested. "We never could."

"Evelyn," I told her, "I am not selling you a diamond ring. I'm giving it to you, at Charlie's request."

Well, that made her cry even more, but the tears were happier now, and she gave me a big hug when we parted company at JFK airport.

When I got back to Houston I put together a modest, but very nice, diamond engagement ring and mailed it to Evelyn at the address in upstate New York she'd given me. Putting that package in the mail made me feel like a million dollars. No, better than that.

Six months later I received a small package at my Houston office. When I opened it, I found the diamond ring I'd sent to Evelyn Benson. With the ring was a note from her daughter:

"Dear Mr. Cuellar, I'm returning the ring which you so graciously allowed my mother to wear for the last six months. Not a day went by that she didn't show it to someone, proud as can be. She told people it was a gift from her late husband Charlie (my Dad). I'd never seen her as happy with anything in my life. My mother passed away last week, so I am returning your ring with many thanks for the joy you brought my mother. Sincerely, Jane Adams."

There are many ways to measure success in this world, my friend, and not all of them involve money.

THE SHERLOCK HOLMES

In Step One, the Treasure Hunt, we located a number of pieces of jewelry we want to sell. Now we have to do a bit of investigative work. We must find out how much our jewelry is really worth, and to do that, we first have to locate another kind of precious gem: The "honest independent appraiser." This may come as a shock to you, but there are dishonest people in the jewelry business. I know, I know—it's hard to believe. The good news is, "Yes, Virginia," there *are* honest appraisers out there. Your mission is to find one. You have to put on your Sherlock Holmes deerstalker cap, follow the clues, use your powers of deductive reasoning, and arrive at the correct conclusion. Elementary, my dear Watson!

But before we set off in search of our honest independent appraiser, I'm going to send you to the back of the book. No, it's not like being sent to the back of the class—you're doing just fine, believe me. In the back of the book, on page 229, you'll find "Fred's Complete Guide to Sorting and Cleaning Jewelry."

The reason is that before you take your jewels to market, you gotta shine 'em up real good so they're looking their best.

Go to page 229.

Read carefully.

Then come back here.

Good! You're back, with your jewelry all sorted out, clean and sparkling. Let's find an appraiser.

Choosing an Appraiser—We need an appraiser we can trust, and one who won't kill us with fees. During my years in the business, I've learned there are six basic types of appraisers. The first five we want to avoid, and I'll tell you how to identify them.

1. **Non-Certified Appraiser**—This should be a no-brainer. Just about any bozo can hang out a shingle and call himself an appraiser, but what qualifies him to make that claim? Has he attended the Gemological Institute of America? GIA is the *only* accredited institute in the United States that certifies jewelry appraisers. If he has attended GIA, what classes did he pass? To evaluate diamonds, he needs to have passed the GIA course in diamonds and diamond grading. To evaluate diamonds and colored stones, he needs to have passed the colored stones course as well, which

would make him a *gemologist*. If he's gone beyond that, by passing the extension classes and tests, he's become a *graduate gemologist*. What we're looking for is a gemologist or graduate gemologist certified in diamonds and colored stones, and he should have the paperwork to prove it.

2. **Jewelry Store Appraiser**—Even though an appraiser has all of the right credentials, he may still be biased. Remember, we're not just looking for an honest appraiser—we're looking for an *independent* honest appraiser. If the guy works in a store that sells jewelry, there are natural economic forces at work that put pressure on him to appraise the stuff they *sell* at the highest possible price, and to appraise the stuff they *buy* at the lowest possible price. So when you take your diamond rings to this guy and ask for an appraisal, he might ask you, "What for?" You tell him you're going to sell the rings, and he thinks, "Hmmm, maybe he'll sell them to me, and I can resell them." So instead of giving you an honest appraisal, he lowballs it to maximize his profit when he resells the merchandise. It's much better to pick an appraiser who isn't going to buy and resell your jewelry, so Fred's advice is, avoid jewelry store appraisers.

3. **Sandbag Appraisers**—Right away you can tell that this sounds like a person to avoid, right? Not that anyone *calls* himself a sandbag appraiser, but there are quite a few who deserve the name. What a sandbagger is, is someone who has a hidden agenda. He deliberately lies about the quality of your jewelry in the hope of making money off it—even if he claims that he doesn't sell jewelry himself.

Here's how the sandbagger works: You take your rings and things to Joe's Honest Appraisal Service, because the sign in the window says he doesn't sell jewelry. He gives you an appraisal, which you think is low. He says, "No, that's what it's worth. I just call 'em as I see 'em. By the way, if you're thinking about selling this stuff, I know a jeweler who might be interested." Aha! He's shown his true colors. Chances are, Joe's got a little backdoor deal going with this jeweler, and he's lowballed your goods in return for a percentage of the profit when the jewelry is resold. If an appraiser ever offers to buy your jewelry, or recommends a jeweler, take your jewelry and run! He's unethical, and you want nothing to do with him.

4. **Percentage Appraiser**—Duh! How dumb do we look? This is a guy who wants to charge us a percentage of the value of the goods, as his fee for doing the appraisal. For example, he tells you your diamond ring is worth $10,000 and his fee is 1%, or $100. Three things are very wrong with this scenario: (1) any appraiser who charges on this basis is bound to inflate the value of your jewelry, which means that (2) you won't know the true value of your jewelry, and (3) you'll be consistently overcharged for his services. Avoid the percentage appraiser.

5. **The Dirty Trickster**—Some appraisers are so dishonest they'll actually try to steal your jewels. Here's Fred's list of the "Top 10 Dirty Appraiser Tricks," or DAT, for short. Remember: DAT's not nice!

Trick #1: "Come back later." The appraiser says, "Thanks for coming in. I'm very busy right now, so you'll have to leave your jewelry and come back to pick it up later along with the appraisal." Why? So he can switch our diamonds for fakes? No way, José! Any appraiser who asks you to leave your jewels with him may be up to something. See you later.

Trick #2: "Gotta pop it." You sit down with the appraiser, he picks up his jeweler's loupe (a magnifying device) and studies your diamond ring for a moment, and then announces, "We're going to have to pop it." "Pop it?" you ask. "Yep. Gotta pop this stone out of the setting so we can take a better look. Otherwise I can't grade it or weigh it properly." Bzzzzzz! Crook alert! The only reason he would want to remove the diamond from its setting is to pull a switcheroo! Any good appraiser can do an accurate enough appraisal with the stone in the setting. Don't let an appraiser "pop" your diamonds.

Trick #3: Free Cleaning. For starters, your jewelry should already be clean. Remember, we sorted and cleaned everything before taking it to the appraiser. An appraiser shouldn't offer to reclean it, unless he does it right in front of you. If he tells you he has to take it into the back room, an alarm bell should go off in your head. Tell him you'd like to accompany him, because you want to keep your jewelry in sight. If he objects, it's time to leave.

Trick #4: "You've been robbed!" The appraiser takes a quick glance at your jewelry and whispers urgently, "You've been robbed! Taken to the cleaners! This stuff is practically worthless." Well, guess what? *He's* probably the crook. First, an honest appraiser will study the jewelry carefully and not rush the appraisal. An appraiser who's in a rush is probably in a hurry to separate you from your jewels for less than they're worth. The next thing he'll probably say is, "I know a jeweler who (could take these off your hands)(could give you a better deal)." At this point, it's time for *you* to rush—out of this guy's shop.

Trick #5: Clients in the Waiting Room. Believe it or not, there are appraisers who won't allow you to accompany your jewelry during the appraisal and ask you to wait in the waiting room. What a crook! His reasoning is generally due to security. He'll tell you that he has a lot of clients' jewelry laying around in his lab and for that reason you can't come back. I repeat again, your jewelry *never leaves your sight*. If an appraiser tries to do anything to separate you from your jewels, he's up to something. A good appraiser will always put your needs first, and always attempt to satisfy your needs.

Trick #6: Stupid Is as Stupid Does. Sometimes when we think an appraiser is a crook, he may be just an idiot. But you never know when an appraiser does something stupid if he's *playing* dumb or really *is* dumb. Either way, he's not someone you want to entrust with your valuable jewelry. For example, if the appraiser looks at your diamond and tells you the color grade, he's either stupid or faking it. No one has color memory good enough to do that. To grade the color, he must use a master set, usually consisting of four to eight pregraded diamonds. Your diamond is compared with the master set. If the appraiser doesn't use a master set or a fabulous piece pf equipment called a colorimeter (that is twice as accurate as the human eye for color grading), we've entered the Dumb Zone and should leave immediately.

Trick #7: The Armchair Appraisal. One of the most important functions an appraiser can perform is to plot, or map, the imperfections of your diamond on a diagram. The imperfections are like fingerprints—they can help identify the diamond, and plotting them helps in the clarity grading. If the appraiser doesn't plot the diamond, but only speaks in generalities such as "It's a clean stone," or "This diamond is good quality," he's not telling us anything useful. He's being a lazy bum. We need precise information so we can properly evaluate our jewelry.

Trick #8: The Armchair Appraisal II. I can't tell you how many lazy appraisers I've seen who pick up a piece of jewelry, hold it in their hand for a few moments, moving the hand up and down, and pronounce, "This weighs about a half an ounce." I don't know *anyone* who can determine the precise weight of a piece of jewelry that way! If an appraiser does that little routine for you, tell him you're not interested in how much he *guesses* it weighs. The only way to weigh jewelry is on a jeweler's scale. Make him use one.

Trick #9: The Broken Promise. The appraiser has quoted you a fee for his services. Between $25 to $50 is a fair price for one piece. Now he tells you, "Gee, I know I said I'd charge $30, but I didn't know what a beautiful, complicated piece of jewelry you had. This is going to take me twice as long as I thought it would, so I'm going to have to raise my fee." Uh-uh. In this business, a quote is a quote. Either he sticks with it, or you walk.

Trick #10: The High Horse. Don't let your appraiser get on his. High horse, that is. Even though your transaction with the appraiser may be brief, during that time he's *your appraiser.* If you have questions, ask them. If you have concerns, say so. And if the appraiser gets all huffy and defensive, that should trigger a warning bell in your head. For example, if you ask for the Rapaport value of the diamonds and the appraiser says that's none of your business, just say, "Well, then I guess my diamonds are none of your business, either," and split.

6. **Independent Appraiser**—Eureka! This is what we've been searching for: An appraiser with the proper GIA certification who is independent from any and all jewelry buyers/sellers; who charges a flat rate (as I mentioned earlier, between $25 and $50 is a fair fee for one piece, and a good appraiser will often discount the fee for additional pieces); and who doesn't try to pull any of the stunts which would brand him as a sandbagger or a dirty trickster. Once he's passed all these tests, you still have a few ground rules you'll want to cover with him:

   a. On every piece of jewelry you want to know the *wholesale value*, not the retail or replacement value.

   b. If a piece of jewelry isn't worth over $250, you don't want it appraised. You'll spend more for the appraisal fee than you'll make on the sale.

   c. You don't want costume jewelry or gold-plated jewelry appraised.

   d. You want the *weight* of the gold, in grams, of each piece of jewelry.

   e. You want the appraiser to tell you the *purity* of the gold in karats—for example, 14 karat gold is $^{14}/_{24}$ pure gold.

   f. The appraiser must tell you the *clarity and color grades* of all diamonds, according to GIA standards.

(These grades and their meanings are explained later in this book.)

g. You want the approximate *weights* of all the diamonds and colored stones.

h. Ask for all the diamonds to be *plotted*.

i. Ask for the *wholesale value* of all colored stones in the jewelry.

j. Ask for the *quality* of the colored stones—are they industrial, commercial gem, or investment quality?

Let's keep in mind what we're doing here. We have accumulated from various sources—safe deposit box, jewelry box, and so forth—some jewelry items which we want to convert into cash. We didn't go out and buy this stuff with the intention of selling it for a profit. So the best we can hope for is to get the so-called dump value of each piece. Remember, we defined dump value in the beginning of the book as the *immediate cash liquidity value* of the jewelry. It's that cold, hard, no-nonsense, bottom-line number that is the highest figure a jeweler will pay for your merchandise. Note that I said the *highest* figure—don't be surprised if the jeweler offers you *less* than dump value. He'll try to pry it away from you for less, because that will increase his margin when he resells the piece. But if you walk in already *knowing* the dump value, you won't get shortchanged.

How do we determine the dump value of a piece of jewelry? By knowing the size and quality of the gem, and the weight and purity of its setting. That's what we paid the appraiser for, to give us those specific pieces of information.

With that information in hand, we turn to the **dump value tables** in this section and find the dollar value of the jewelry.

To read the dump value tables, you need to understand the abbreviations for the color and clarity grades. These grades are established by the Gemological Institute of America and are recognized internationally as the grading standards for diamonds and colored stones.

Color—Color grades for diamonds are letters ranging from D to Z, with most diamonds on the market falling into the G-to-M range. As the letters go down the alphabet, the diamonds go from pure white through various shades of yellow. Grades of D-E-F are clear white, and quite rare and valuable (there are slight differences between the letter grades in each group). At the other end of the alphabet, a Z-grade diamond is a rare colored diamond, or "fancy" stone. For example, a Z-grade might be the bright yellow stone called a "canary," very rare and valuable. Here is the GIA color-grading scale:

D-E-F	Colorless
G-H-I	Nearly colorless
J-K-L	Slightly yellow
M-N-O	Light yellow
P through X	Progressively darker yellow
Z	Fancy colors

Clarity—This means how clear, or free, the diamond is of blemishes and inclusions when viewed with the naked eye or a jeweler's loupe (magnifier). *Blemishes* are imperfections on the outside of the stone such as chips or scratches. *Inclusions* are internal flaws such as little black spots caused by carbon deposits, or internal cracks. Flawless diamonds are very rare and very expensive. Most diamonds on the market have blemishes and/or inclusions, but if they can't be seen with the naked eye, the stone is called "eye clean" and is considered a fairly good diamond. Following are the GIA clarity grades:

Flawless	Free of inclusions and blemishes when viewed under a loupe. *Very rare, very expensive.*
Internally flawless	Free of inclusions; may have minor blemishes visible under a loupe. *Very rare and very expensive.*
VVS-1, VVS-2	Very, very slightly included. Flaws no bigger than a pinpoint when seen under a loupe. *Rare and expensive.*
VS-1, VS-2	Very slightly included. Flaws smaller than a grain of salt when viewed under a loupe. *High quality.*
SI-1	Slightly included. "Eye clean." *Good quality.*
SI-2	Slightly included. Some flaws visible to the naked eye. *Borderline quality.*

I-1, I-2, I-3   Imperfect. Inclusions and blemishes visible to the naked eye. *Commercial grade.*

Now you know the abbreviations for color grade and clarity grade. Find the dump value table for the correct size of your diamond, and you can easily determine the dump value. And, using the formulas **Dump = 60% of Wholesale,** and **Retail = 2 × Wholesale,** you can also determine the wholesale and approximate retail value of the diamond. Let's walk through it with this chart, which is for ⅓ carat diamonds:

⅓ CARAT

COLOR	IF	VVS-1	VVS-2	VS-1	SI-1	SI-2	I-1	I-2	I-3
D	1,009	950	891	672	585	455	316	257	198
E	950	891	792	693	534	435	297	237	178
F	891	792	732	633	495	415	277	217	178
G	772	670	633	574	475	396	257	217	158
H	594	554	514	475	415	376	237	198	158
I	475	455	435	415	376	356	237	198	158
J	415	415	396	376	336	316	217	198	138
K	376	356	336	316	297	277	217	175	138
L	336	316	336	277	277	257	178	158	138
M	297	297	277	257	237	257	158	138	138

Let's say you have a ⅓ carat diamond, and the honest independent appraiser tells you the clarity is I-2 and the color grade is G. Go to the G line on the left, follow that line over to the I-2 column, and you'll see that the dump value of your diamond is $217. In other words, that's the diamond's cash value to you, and the lowest price you should accept for it.

To determine what the diamond's *wholesale* price would be, divide $217 by .60 (because the dump value is 60% of wholesale) and you get $361.66.

And using the formula, **Retail = 2 × Wholesale**, you can determine that the retail price of your diamond would be around $723.33. (I say "around" because retail prices vary so much.)

That's all there is to it. Following are other dump value tables for diamonds from ½ carat to 5 carats. Use them to find your lowest selling price:

½ CARAT

COLOR	IF	VVS-1	VVS-2	VS-1	VS-2	SI-1	SI-2	I-1	I-2	I-3
D	2,490	2,040	1,800	1,530	1,260	1,080	870	690	540	420
E	2,040	1,890	1,620	1,440	1,230	1,050	840	660	510	390
F	1,890	1,650	1,470	1,350	1,200	990	810	630	480	390
G	1,650	1,470	1,350	1,290	1,140	930	780	600	480	360
H	1,410	1,290	1,170	1,110	990	900	750	570	450	360
I	1,140	1,050	990	900	840	780	720	540	450	360
J	960	900	840	810	780	750	690	510	450	330
K	780	750	720	690	660	630	570	480	420	330
L	750	720	690	660	630	600	540	420	390	300
M	630	600	600	570	540	510	480	390	360	270

Example: a ½ ct, VS-1, D's dump value is $1,530.

¾ CARAT

COLOR	IF	VVS-1	VVS-2	VS-1	VS-2	SI-1	SI-2	I-1	I-2	I-3
D	4,005	3,195	2,880	2,475	2,160	1,980	1,755	1,260	900	675
E	3,195	2,970	2,565	2,295	2,070	1,935	1,710	1,260	900	630
F	2,925	2,610	2,295	2,115	2,025	1,890	1,665	1,260	855	630
G	2,565	2,340	2,115	2,025	1,935	1,800	1,620	1,230	855	585
H	2,295	2,115	2,025	1,935	1,845	1,710	1,530	1,170	810	585
I	1,935	1,845	1,800	1,755	1,620	1,620	1,440	1,125	765	585
J	1,710	1,620	1,620	1,575	1,485	1,395	1,305	1,080	765	540
K	1,530	1,485	1,440	1,395	1,305	1,215	1,125	900	720	540
L	1,305	1,260	1,215	1,170	1,170	1,080	990	720	630	495
M	1,080	1,080	1,035	1,035	1,035	990	900	675	585	450

Example: a ¾ ct, VS-1, G's dump value is $2,025.

1 CARAT

COLOR	IF	VVS-1	VVS-2	VS-1	VS-2	SI-1	SI-2	I-1	I-2	I-3
D	9,600	6,660	5,760	4,680	3,900	3,420	3,060	2,220	1,560	1,080
E	6,660	5,820	4,680	4,080	3,780	3,360	3,000	2,160	1,560	1,020
F	5,820	4,800	4,140	3,960	3,660	3,330	2,940	2,100	1,500	1,020
G	4,740	4,200	3,900	3,720	3,480	3,240	2,880	2,040	1,440	960
H	4,140	3,780	3,600	3,420	3,300	3,120	2,760	1,860	1,380	960
I	3,660	3,480	3,300	3,180	3,060	2,880	2,580	1,920	1,320	900
J	3,360	3,240	3,120	3,000	2,880	2,640	2,400	1,800	1,260	900
K	3,060	2,940	2,880	2,760	2,580	2,460	2,220	1,680	1,200	840
L	2,580	2,520	2,460	2,340	2,220	2,100	1,980	1,560	1,140	780
M	2,160	2,100	2,040	1,920	1,860	1,680	1,560	1,320	1,080	780

Example: a 1 ct, SI-1, I's dump value is $2,880.

1½ CARAT

COLOR	IF	VVS-1	VVS-2	VS-1	VS-2	SI-1	SI-2	I-1	I-2	I-3
D	15,750	10,890	9,900	8,280	6,750	5,760	5,220	3,690	2,610	1,710
E	10,890	9,990	8,370	7,020	6,480	5,670	4,950	3,600	2,610	1,620
F	9,990	8,550	7,290	6,660	6,210	5,580	4,860	3,510	2,520	1,620
G	8,460	7,290	6,570	6,300	5,850	5,400	4,770	3,510	2,430	1,530
H	7,200	6,390	6,030	5,850	5,580	5,310	4,590	3,420	2,340	1,530
I	6,120	5,850	5,580	5,400	5,130	4,770	4,320	3,300	2,250	1,440
J	5,670	5,490	5,220	5,130	4,860	4,500	4,050	3,060	2,160	1,440
K	5,130	4,950	4,770	4,590	4,320	4,050	3,690	2,790	2,070	1,350
L	4,320	4,140	4,050	3,870	3,690	3,510	3,240	2,610	1,980	1,260
M	3,960	3,510	3,420	3,240	3,060	2,790	2,610	2,250	1,800	1,260

Example: a 1½ ct, VVS-2, J's dump value is $5,220.

2 CARAT

COLOR	IF	VVS-1	VVS-2	VS-1	VS-2	SI-1	SI-2	I-1	I-2	I-3
D	30,000	23,040	20,040	15,840	16,960	9,840	7,920	5,400	3,720	2,520
E	23,040	20,040	15,840	13,680	11,400	9,600	7,800	5,280	3,720	2,400
F	20,040	15,960	14,100	11,760	10,920	9,360	7,680	5,160	3,720	2,280
G	15,840	14,160	11,640	10,920	10,200	8,880	7,440	5,040	3,600	2,280
H	13,560	11,400	10,560	9,960	9,000	8,160	7,080	4,920	3,480	2,160
I	10,440	9,840	9,480	8,520	7,800	7,320	6,600	4,800	3,360	2,040
J	9,120	8,760	8,280	7,680	7,200	6,720	6,000	4,680	3,240	2,040
K	7,560	7,320	7,080	6,840	6,600	6,120	5,520	4,320	3,120	1,920
L	6,360	6,120	5,880	5,640	5,400	5,160	4,800	3,960	3,000	1,800
M	5,400	5,160	4,920	4,680	4,440	4,080	3,840	3,360	2,760	1,800

Example: a 2 ct, IF, G's dump value is $15,840.

3 CARAT

COLOR	IF	VVS-1	VVS-2	VS-1	VS-2	SI-1	SI-2	I-1	I-2	I-3
D	71,100	51,660	43,560	33,660	27,360	22,500	16,740	12,600	6,840	4,140
E	51,660	44,640	33,840	27,360	24,300	21,060	15,840	11,700	6,660	3,960
F	43,560	34,020	27,540	24,300	22,680	19,620	15,120	10,980	6,480	3,780
G	33,660	27,540	24,300	22,680	19,620	17,460	14,220	10,440	6,120	3,600
H	27,360	24,120	22,140	19,800	17,460	14,940	13,320	9,720	5,760	3,600
I	21,420	19,620	18,720	16,900	14,760	13,500	11,500	9,000	5,580	3,420
J	17,820	16,920	16,200	14,760	13,320	12,240	10,980	8,280	5,220	3,240
K	15,840	14,940	14,220	12,960	11,880	10,800	9,540	7,740	5,040	3,240
L	12,420	11,880	11,340	10,800	9,900	8,820	7,740	6,300	4,860	3,060
M	10,080	9,720	9,360	9,000	8,640	7,740	6,840	5,580	4,500	3,060

Example: a 3 ct, VVS-1, H's dump value is $24,120.

4 CARAT

COLOR	IF	VVS-1	VVS-2	VS-1	VS-2	SI-1	SI-2	I-1	I-2	I-3
D	99,600	73,680	62,880	48,480	40,080	33,120	2,4000	18,240	10,320	5,760
E	73,680	62,880	48,480	40,080	37,200	30,720	22,800	17,040	10,080	5,520
F	62,880	48,720	37,620	35,280	32,880	38,320	21,840	16,080	9,600	5,280
G	48,480	40,320	35,520	32,880	28,560	24,720	20,880	14,520	9,360	5,040
H	38,880	35,280	31,680	28,560	29,700	22,320	19,200	14,160	8,880	5,040
I	30,480	28,080	26,160	24,960	23,040	19,920	17,760	13,440	8,400	4,800
J	24,480	23,280	22,080	20,880	19,680	17,520	16,080	12,480	7,920	4,560
K	21,600	20,400	19,200	18,000	16,800	15,120	13,920	11,040	7,440	4,320
L	17,280	16,320	15,840	15,120	14,160	12,720	11,280	9,360	6,960	4,080
M	14,400	13,680	13,440	12,960	12,480	11,000	10,080	8,400	6,480	4,080

Example: a 4 ct, VVS-1, I's dump value is $28,080.

5 CARAT

COLOR	IF	VVS-1	VVS-2	VS-1	VS-2	SI-1	SI-2	I-1	I-2	I-3
D	166,500	117,600	99,600	83,100	68,100	57,900	39,900	24,900	14,700	8,100
E	117,600	101,100	83,100	71,100	62,100	51,900	38,400	23,400	14,700	7,500
F	101,100	83,400	72,900	63,600	54,600	45,900	36,900	22,500	13,500	7,200
G	83,100	72,900	63,900	54,600	48,000	41,700	34,500	21,300	12,900	6,900
H	69,600	62,100	54,600	48,000	42,300	35,700	29,700	19,800	12,300	6,600
I	54,600	51,600	48,000	41,700	36,900	29,700	26,100	18,000	11,700	6,300
J	38,400	36,900	35,400	33,300	30,000	25,200	22,500	16,500	11,100	6,000
K	30,900	29,400	27,900	26,400	24,900	22,200	18,900	15,000	10,500	6,000
L	25,200	23,700	21,900	21,300	19,800	18,300	15,600	13,200	9,600	5,700
M	20,700	20,100	18,900	18,000	17,100	15,900	14,100	11,400	8,700	5,700

Example: a 5 ct, IF, D's dump value is $166,500.

Gold Dumping—Most, if not all, of the jewelry you own is made of gold or platinum. Just as diamonds have dump values, so do gold and platinum. Their dump values are based on weight, which is measured in grams, and the purity of the gold, which is measured in *karats*. The appraiser has told you the weights and purity of your jewelry, so you're ready to use the **gold/platinum** table on page 30.

The prices in the left-hand column reflect the *current market price per ounce* of the pure metal. Since that price fluctuates daily, you'll need to get the current figure from your daily newspaper's financial section. The other columns are adjusted to reflect the karat weight of the gold minus a discount that the gold dealer will charge when he purchases your gold. The gold and platinum dealer typically keeps 3 to 5% as his fee.

GOLD/PLATINUM DUMP VALUE TABLE (PRICE PER GRAM)

CURRENT MARKET PRICE PER TROY OUNCE	10K	14K	18K	PLATINUM
$300.00	$3.81	$5.34	$6.87	$9.16
$310.00	$3.94	$5.52	$7.10	$9.46
$320.00	$4.07	$5.70	$7.33	$9.77
$330.00	$4.20	$5.88	$7.56	$10.08
$340.00	$4.33	$6.06	$7.85	$10.38
$350.00	$4.45	$6.24	$8.02	$10.69
$360.00	$4.58	$6.42	$8.25	$10.99
$370.00	$4.70	$6.60	$8.48	$11.30
$380.00	$4.83	$6.78	$8.71	$11.60
$390.00	$4.96	$6.96	$8.94	$11.91
$400.00	$5.09	$7.14	$9.17	$12.21
$410.00	$5.22	$7.32	$9.40	$12.52
$420.00	$5.35	$7.50	$9.63	$12.82
$430.00	$5.48	$7.68	$9.86	$13.13
$440.00	$5.61	$7.86	$10.09	$13.44
$450.00	$5.74	$8.04	$10.32	$13.74
$460.00	$5.87	$8.22	$10.55	$14.05
$470.00	$6.00	$8.40	$10.78	$14.35
$480.00	$6.13	$8.58	$11.01	$14.66
$490.00	$6.26	$8.76	$11.24	$14.96
$500.00	$6.39	$8.94	$11.47	$15.27
$510.00	$6.52	$9.12	$11.70	$15.57
$520.00	$6.65	$9.30	$11.93	$15.88
$530.00	$6.78	$9.48	$12.16	$16.19
$540.00	$6.91	$9.66	$12.39	$16.49
$550.00	$7.04	$9.84	$12.62	$16.80
$560.00	$7.13	$10.02	$12.85	$17.10
$570.00	$7.26	$10.20	$13.08	$17.41

GOLD/PLATINUM DUMP VALUE TABLE *(CONTINUED)*

CURRENT MARKET PRICE PER TROY OUNCE	10K	14K	18K	PLATINUM
$580.00	$7.39	$10.38	$13.31	$17.71
$590.00	$7.52	$10.56	$13.54	$18.02
$600.00	$7.65	$10.74	$13.77	$18.32
$610.00	$7.78	$10.92	$14.00	$18.63
$620.00	$7.91	$11.10	$14.23	$18.93
$630.00	$8.04	$11.28	$14.46	$19.24
$640.00	$8.17	$11.46	$14.69	$19.55
$650.00	$8.30	$11.64	$14.92	$19.85
$660.00	$8.43	$11.82	$15.15	$20.16
$670.00	$8.56	$12.00	$15.38	$20.46
$680.00	$8.69	$12.18	$15.61	$20.77
$690.00	$8.82	$12.36	$15.84	$21.07
$700.00	$8.95	$12.54	$16.07	$21.38
$710.00	$9.08	$12.72	$16.30	$21.68
$720.00	$9.21	$12.90	$16.53	$21.99
$730.00	$9.34	$13.08	$16.76	$22.29
$740.00	$9.47	$13.26	$16.99	$22.60
$750.00	$9.60	$13.44	$17.22	$22.91
$760.00	$9.73	$13.62	$17.45	$23.21
$770.00	$9.86	$13.80	$17.68	$23.52
$780.00	$9.99	$13.98	$17.91	$23.82
$790.00	$10.12	$14.16	$18.14	$24.13
$800.00	$10.25	$14.34	$18.37	$24.43

Example 1: Let's say you're selling a 14K yellow gold chain that weighs 15 grams. You check the paper and find that today's market price for gold is $360 per ounce. On the left-hand side of the chart, go down the current market price column to $360.

31

Follow that line over to the 14K column, and you see that the dump value *per gram* is $6.42. Multiply that by 15, which is the weight of your jewelry:

$$15 \times 6.42 = 96.30$$

The dump value of the item is $96.30. (By the way, 1 troy ounce = 31.1 grams.)

Example 2: Your next item of jewelry is an 18K ring that weighs 10 grams. You find that today's market price for pure gold is $440 per ounce (it's gone up dramatically since you sold the chain in Example 1). Go down the current market price column to the $440 line, and follow that line over to the 18K column. There you find the dump value is $10.09 per gram:

$$10 \times 10.09 = 100.90$$

The dump value of your ring is $100.90.

Keep in mind that the dump values of precious metals are based *solely on weight and purity*. There is no consideration for the beauty or intricacy of the jewelry when you're liquidating the stuff—it's purely a commodity transaction, and what the dealer is paying for is the *bullion value*, or the amount of pure gold in the piece. The "current market price" is just that—what the market is paying at this moment for an ounce of pure gold bullion. Because of this, gold jewelry is just slightly better than, say, Louisiana swampland as an investment. Come dump time, it's worth no more than its pure gold content. So next time you go shopping for a piece of gold jewelry, ask for the gram weight of the article and calculate the dump price. If they're charging more than twice the dump price, you should shop elsewhere.

Colored Stone Dumping—Three out of four people who get engaged buy an engagement ring. Ninety-five percent of those rings are diamond rings. That's why there is a strong secondary market for diamonds, and that's why this book is called *Diamonds for Profit* and not *Colored Stones for Profit*. Colored stones are beautiful, but they are really tough to resell. The demand simply isn't there, and the fact that a lot of colored stones are now man-made has weakened the market even further. That said, they do have *some* dump value. Before looking at the tables, let's go over the lingo jewelers use in discussing the top three colored stones: Ruby, emerald, and sapphire.

Cabochon—A gemstone cut having a rounded dome and a flat base. Imagine cutting a marble in half—each half would be a cabochon.

Facet—a flat surface on a polished gemstone. The facets on gemstones refract and disperse light, enhancing the stone's beauty.

Hue (pronounced "hYOU")—This is just another word for color, as in, "Your nose has a lovely red hue."

Tone—How light or dark a particular hue is. Think of robin's egg blue, sky blue, and navy blue as three tones of blue, from light to dark.

Saturation—Describes the richness, vibrancy, or intensity of the color. If I told you a stone was an "electric sky blue" or a "dull sky blue," I'd be describing the saturation (electric or dull), the tone (sky), and the hue (blue).

Transparent—If a gemstone allows light to pass through it, and allows you to see into it, it is transparent.

Opaque—The opposite of transparent. The stone does *not* allow light to pass through.

Milky—Translucent. Cloudy, foggy. Somewhere between transparent and opaque. Allows some light to pass through, but you can't see through it.

Window—If a gemstone has a window, this means that it is transparent and cut shallow, so you cannot only see into it, but see right through it to whatever's on the other side. Just like a—window!

Country of Origin—In diamonds, country of origin means little or nothing. In colored stones, it can mean a lot. The best rubies come from Burma, and the best sapphires from Kashmir, so on the chart I've separated them from regular rubies and sapphires. *Most* of the world's good emeralds come from Colombia, so I haven't separated them.

RUBY DUMP VALUE TABLE

**	INVESTMENT (EXCELLENT)*	GEM (VERY GOOD)	COMMERCIAL (SATISFACTORY)	INDUSTRIAL (POOR)
¼ CT MC	—	20–34	15–25	3–6
EC	—	24–30	12–22	3–4
NEC	—	12–24	9–7	2–3
⅓ CT MC	—	57–82	49–66	24–33
EC	—	47–71	36–53	21–28
NEC	—	37–53	30–41	14–18

*Note: Where a dash is present and no price is given, quantities are in such limited numbers that there is no dump price available.
**MC—Microscope Clean.
EC—Eye Clean.
NEC—Not Eye Clean.

RUBY DUMP VALUE TABLE *(CONTINUED)*

**		INVESTMENT (EXCELLENT)*	GEM (VERY GOOD)	COMMERCIAL (SATISFACTORY)	INDUSTRIAL (POOR)
½ CT	MC	—	166–218	107–137	40–56
	EC	—	142–187	97–112	35–50
	NEC	—	109–146	68–93	25–32
⅞ CT	MC	—	630–826	435–652	130–152
	EC	—	565–739	391–565	113–130
	NEC	—	413–510	304–413	87–104
1 CT	MC	—	1,125–1,575	750–1,250	200–250
	EC	—	1,025–1,437	650–1,150	162–200
	NEC	—	725–1,050	500–950	115–140
2 CT	MC	—	4,400–5,700	2,800–3,800	800–1,800
	EC	—	3,900–5,150	2,400–3,400	650–800
	NEC	—	2,700–3,800	2,000–3,000	500–600
3 CT	MC	—	7,425–9,525	4,950–6,750	1,800–2,025
	EC	—	6,600–8,625	4,200–6,000	1,350–1,650
	NEC	—	4,725–6,150	3,300–4,800	1,050–1,500
4 CT	MC	—	14,000–17,900	10,000–13,000	3,200–4,000
	EC	—	12,500–14,800	8,800–11,800	2,800–3,600
	NEC	—	9,300–12,000	7,600–10,000	2,400–3,000
5 CT	MC	—	20,000–25,375	15,000–19,500	5,000–6,000
	EC	—	17,625–21,250	11,250–16,500	4,000–5,375
	NEC	—	13,750–17,375	11,500–13,500	3,500–4,500

Example: a 1 ct, gem-quality MC ruby's dump value is between $1,125–$1,575.

Burma Ruby Dump Value Table

••		INVESTMENT (EXCELLENT)	GEM (VERY GOOD)	COMMERCIAL (SATISFACTORY)	INDUSTRIAL (POOR)
½ CT	MC	—	331–437	125–150	75–112
	EC	—	280–375	105–137	68–100
	NEC	—	218–293	77–100	50–62
⅞ CT	MC	—	1,196–1,631	304–348	261–304
	EC	—	1,087–1,479	274–304	226–261
	NEC	—	826–1,022	204–137	174–208
1 CT	MC	—	2,750–3,750	450–650	400–500
	EC	—	2,275–3,275	375–500	325–400
	NEC	—	1,500–2,200	290–410	230–280
2 CT	MC	—	9,750–12,000	3,000–4,500	1,600–2,000
	EC	—	8,400–10,750	2,400–3,700	1,300–1,600
	NEC	—	5,400–7,600	1,800–2,700	1,000–1,200
3 CT	MC	—	19,950–24,000	6,700–8,100	3,600–3,900
	EC	—	15,750–19,125	4,500–6,000	2,700–3,300
	NEC	—	11,025–13,875	3,600–4,950	2,100–3,000
4 CT	MC	—	47,000–62,000	16,000–24,000	6,400–8,000
	EC	—	38,000–47,000	14,000–20,000	5,600–7,200
	NEC	—	27,000–33,000	13,600–14,000	4,800–6,000
5 CT	MC	—	87,500–112,500	25,000–30,000	10,000–12,000
	EC	—	62,500–75,000	22,500–30,000	8,000–10,750
	NEC	—	43,750–53,750	6,000–8,250	3,500–5,000

Example: a 1 ct, NEC, industrial-grade Burmese ruby's dump value is between $230–$280.

BLUE SAPPHIRE DUMP VALUE TABLE

		INVESTMENT (EXCELLENT)	GEM (VERY GOOD)	COMMERCIAL (SATISFACTORY)	INDUSTRIAL (POOR)
¼ CT	MC	—	11–22	6–12	1–4
	EC	—	10–18	5–11	1–3
	NEC	—	7–14	4–8	1–2
⅓ CT	MC	—	26–41	13–23	2–6
	EC	—	23–37	11–19	2–5
	NEC	—	19–31	7–13	1–3
½ CT	MC	—	62–86	25–40	5–12
	EC	—	54–74	21–33	5–11
	NEC	—	45–62	17–25	3–8
⅞ CT	MC	—	146–189	82–108	17–32
	EC	—	123–154	69–91	14–30
	NEC	—	101–135	47–73	13–26
1 CT	MC	500–750	375–512	150–225	37–75
	EC	400–650	325–400	137–187	32–65
	NEC	350–550	262–350	120–170	30–60
2 CT	MC	1,400–1,700	1,000–1,250	424–650	200–324
	EC	1,100–1,400	862–1,100	374–474	160–274
	NEC	900–1,200	712–950	325–400	130–240
3 CT	MC	2,700–3,150	2,025–2,325	861–1,125	225–411
	EC	2,250–2,700	1,725–2,043	786–975	336–465
	NEC	1,650–2,100	1,311–1,575	675–825	261–375
4 CT	MC	5,000–6,000	3,400–4,224	1,400–1,700	800–1,000
	EC	4,000–4,800	3,000–3,448	1,148–1,400	680–880
	NEC	3,000–3,600	2,300–2,648	948–1,300	580–748
5 CT	MC	6,750–7,000	5,000–6,000	3,000–4,000	1,375–1,875
	EC	5,500–6,750	4,500–5,435	2,250–3,000	1,200–1,450
	NEC	3,750–5,000	3,125–4,310	2,000–2,375	1,050–1,250

Example: a 1 ct, EC, commercial sapphire's dump value is between $137–$187.

KASHMIR BLUE SAPPHIRE DUMP VALUE TABLE

		INVESTMENT (EXCELLENT)	GEM (VERY GOOD)	COMMERCIAL (SATISFACTORY)	INDUSTRIAL (POOR)
1.00 CT	MC	3,500–3,775	2,075–2,375	850–1,000	600–700
	EC	2,750–3,000	1,700–1,975	750–950	400–600
	NEC	2,250–2,500	1,450–1,725	600–750	350–550
2.00 CT	MC	10,000–11,000	6,350–7,350	2,400–3,400	1,900–2,200
	EC	8,700–9,900	5,700–6,650	2,100–3,100	1,700–1,900
	NEC	7,200–8,200	4,500–5,250	1,900–2,600	1,500–1,700
3.00 CT	MC	18,750–20,250	12,750–14,250	5,250–6,750	3,750–4,500
	EC	16,500–18,000	11,250–12,750	4,500–6,000	3,300–4,050
	NEC	12,750–13,800	9,375–10,650	3,750–5,250	2,700–3,300
4.00 CT	MC	32,000–34,000	21,000–23,000	13,400–15,000	6,000–8,000
	EC	28,000–30,000	18,500–20,500	12,400–14,000	5,400–7,200
	NEC	6,000–6,500	15,200–16,800	10,400–11,800	5,000–6,600

Example: a 1 ct, NEC, gem Kashmir sapphire's dump value is between $1,450–$1,725.

EMERALD DUMP VALUE TABLE

		INVESTMENT (EXCELLENT)	GEM (VERY GOOD)	COMMERCIAL (SATISFACTORY)	INDUSTRIAL (POOR)
¼ CT	MC	75–81	62–75	—	—
	EC	62–68	53–62	—	—
	NEC	50–59	43–50	—	—
⅓ CT	MC	214–247	181–206	—	—
	EC	181–222	165–189	—	—
	NEC	165–198	148–165	—	—
½ CT	MC	550–650	387–462	175–225	95–112
	EC	475–562	325–390	150–200	68–87
	NEC	425–500	287–346	125–181	62–81
⅞ CT	MC	1,653–1,870	1,044–1,211	435–543	217–249
	EC	1,261–1,500	848–957	391–478	162–195
	NEC	1,131–1,348	739–863	348–413	140–174
1.00 CT	MC	3,250–3,750	1,950–2,275	800–900	375–412
	EC	2,600–3,100	1,550–1,825	650–750	212–250
	NEC	2,350–2,850	1,375–1,637	600–687	200–225
2.00 CT	MC	9,000–10,124	6,100–6,800	3,000–3,450	1,000–1,250
	EC	7,000–7,950	5,000–5,312	2,800–3,124	900–1,000
	NEC	6,400–7,124	3,950–4,624	2,500–2,800	774–874
3.00 CT	MC	18,000–21,000	11,475–12,975	6,900–8,400	3,300–3,750
	EC	14,250–16,800	8,850–10,500	5,700–6,900	2,550–3,000
	NEC	13,500–15,000	2,700–3,150	5,100–6,261	2,400–2,736

Example: a 1 ct, MC, investment emerald's dump value is between $3,250–$3,750.

Review

Before we "Do the Donald" (make the $$$) I'd like to go over the ground again with a few examples to make sure we're all on the same page. Then, *"We're off to see the Wizard"* (not of Oz—I'll explain in Section III).

Example #1 *The Treasure Hunt*—We come up with an old engagement ring and two gold wedding bands.

The Sherlock Holmes—By evaluation and appraisal, we learn the engagement ring *diamond* is a 1-carat, VS-1, G-color. On our dump value tables we find that a 1 ct, VS-1, G diamond has a dump value of $3,720.

We also learn that the *gold* is all 10K and weighs a total of 11 grams. We check the morning paper and find that the current market value of gold bullion is $320 an ounce. On our gold dumping table we see that if the market price is $320, the dump value of one gram of 10K gold is $4.07. We multiply that by 11 grams, which is the total weight of our gold, and come up with the figure of $44.77.

Conclusion—We should get $3,720 for our diamond and $44.77 for our gold, for a total of $3,764.77. Now we're ready to "Do the Donald" for this lot of treasure.

Example #2 *The Treasure Hunt*—This time our search yields a diamond and ruby fashion ring.

The Sherlock Holmes—Evaluation and appraisal reveals the *diamond* is $1/2$ ct, SI-2, J in color. The ring also holds four rubies—not Burmese. Our rubies are classified as MC, "microscope clean" gem, $1/4$ ct each for a total of $4 \times 1/4$ ct = 1 ct total weight. We go to the dumping tables. The dump value for the $1/2$ ct, SI-2, J diamond is $690. The dump value for MC gem rubies, .25 ct is 20 to 34 $\times$ 4 = 80 to 136.

The *gold* is 14K and weighs 3.5 grams. The market price is $400 per ounce, and the dump value of 14K gold is $7.14 per gram.

$$3.5 \text{ grams} \times \$7.14 = \textbf{\$24.99}.$$

Conclusion—Our diamond and ruby ring is worth $690 for the diamond, between $80 and $136 for the rubies, and $24.99 for the gold. If we go low on the rubies, our total dump value is $690 + $80 + $24.99 = $794.99. We're ready to "Do the Donald."

Example #3 *The Treasure Hunt*—We find a pair of diamond studded earrings in platinum mountings.

The Sherlock Holmes—Our honest independent appraiser tells us the *diamonds* are 1 ct each, SI-1, I-color. The table tells us the dump value is $2,880 per diamond for a total of $5,760.

The *platinum* mountings have a total weight of 1 gram. The market price for platinum is $500 per ounce, there are 31.1 grams per ounce, then you subtract the 5% deduction to the gold and platinum dealer.

$500 divided by 31.1 × .95 = **$15.27 per gram**

Conclusion—The diamonds plus the platinum: $5,760 + $15.27 = $5,775.27. And we're ready to "Do the Donald"!

So, to summarize, in Chapter 1: The Treasure Hunt, we gathered the jewelry we wanted to sell. In Chapter 2: The Sherlock Holmes, we investigated the appraisal process, located an honest independent appraiser, and translated the appraisal into dump value or liquidation values. Now we're ready to cash in. That's what we'll learn how to do in Chapter 3, and when you finish that, you'll be ready for *payday!* Onward!

Do As I Say . . .
A Tale of Woe

The guy had called ahead, as my ad told him to, so I was expecting him when he walked into my office that Saturday afternoon. He was a young fella, in his late twenties, I guessed, and he had a bitter sort of expression on his face. I could tell things hadn't been going too well for him, and I admit I felt some sympathy for him right away. He briskly pulled a little package from his coat pocket and handed it to me.

"My engagement ring," he told me, with more than a touch of sarcasm. "It was thrown back in my face two days ago. I want to be rid of it."

Up until two days ago, he must have really loved this woman. The ring was pretty nice. Better than pretty nice, actually. I guesstimated the stone at 2 ct, VVS-1, F color. I figured the stone had a dump value of $15,960. The young man's purchase receipt validated my calculations. He had paid $33,000 for the ring two months earlier.

But since this was an expensive stone, and I do have my standards, I told him I wanted to pull the stone before I made my decision.

"No!" he said, quite forcefully. "I'm only asking $10,000, and you can take it or leave it. I don't want to risk damaging the stone. If you can't see already that this is a good deal, I'll take it to someone else."

It *was* a good deal. Or so it appeared. If the part of the stone I couldn't see was as gorgeous as the 99% I *could* see, this was a no-brainer. I could dump the diamond quickly and make over $5,000 for a few minutes' work. If I didn't take it, the guy would walk. Dollar signs flashed in my eyes. They blinded me.

I paid the man his $10,000 and he quickly left. As soon as he did, I pulled the stone and found the ugly chipping around the girdle. My heart sinking, I placed the diamond on my scale: 1.87 carats. In the space of ten minutes I'd gone from being $5,000 richer to being $5,000 poorer. All because I disobeyed one of my own cardinal rules.

". . . not greedy of filthy lucre; but patient . . ." *(I Timothy, 2)*

CHAPTER THREE

"DOING THE DONALD"

O kay, we're ready for the most exciting and rewarding part of the whole process: *Making money!* Most people who are doing this for the first time are babes in the woods. They simply take their old jewelry into the nearest jewelry store and innocently throw themselves at the mercy of the jeweler, thinking—hoping, praying!—that this nice man will surely give them the best possible price. Right. That's like jumping into the shark tank after cutting yourself shaving. They'll be lucky if they walk out of there with their clothes on, not to mention their jewelry.

But *you* have now gone to school with Fred, and you are armed with the world's most dangerous weapon: Knowledge. You know what you're holding in your hot little hand, and you know to the penny what it's worth. Armed with that knowledge, you're not going to lose! You'll feel like Donald Trump does when he sets off to negotiate a mega-million-dollar deal.

"We're off to see the Wizard!"—What's this "wizard" stuff, Fred? Remember how Dorothy and Toto, the Cowardly Lion, the Tin Man, and the Scarecrow set off toward the Emerald City to see the Wizard of Oz? They each wanted the Wizard

to grant them a wish, and each knew exactly what he or she wanted—a heart for the Tin Man, a brain for the Scarecrow, "c-c-c-courage" for the Lion, and a trip back to Kansas for Dorothy and Toto. When they reached Oz, they discovered that the Wizard was just a little man behind a curtain.

That's how I want you to approach your jewelry transactions. You know exactly what you want, because you've done the evaluation and appraisal work and calculated your selling price. And I don't want you to be intimidated by a buyer who huffs and puffs and roars that your merchandise isn't worth that much. *Just think of that buyer as a little man behind a curtain* and stand up to him just as Dorothy did to the Wizard of Oz! So when I say, "We're off to see the Wizard," that's how I want you to think of the buyers. But don't forget: In the end, the Tin Man got a heart, the Scarecrow got a brain, the Lion got c-c-c-courage, and Dorothy got home to Kansas and her Auntie Em. So you also have to believe that in the end, the Wizard will make your dreams come true.

There are many types of wizards, but for the moment we'll concern ourselves with three: *Jewelers, wholesalers and dealers clubs,* and *pawnbrokers.*

Wizard #1—The Jeweler

Normally, jewelers purchase diamonds and jewelry at 20 to 25% below wholesale. So you can bet they're going to want to buy *your* merchandise at a 40% discount, or 60% of wholesale—which is dump value. Chances are that you'll be offered even *less* than dump value. Some jewelers will try to sandbag you and tell you your jewelry isn't worth what you think it is. But don't forget: You're "Doing the Donald," and you walked in there not *thinking* but *knowing* exactly what your stuff is worth. As soon as the jeweler realizes that, he'll probably pay you what you're asking. If he won't, don't worry—someone else will.

Before you actually go to a jeweler, *call ahead* to see if he buys jewelry and to make an appointment. No sense wasting time and shoe leather visiting jewelers with no money.

Be patient. You may have to visit five or six jewelers before you get your price, but *you will get your price.*

WARNING!
Two things to beware of at the jeweler's!

Warning #1: The Consignment Scam—A lot of jewelers will try to get you to leave your jewelry with them *on consignment,* telling you you'll get more money that way. Forget about it! If you leave your stuff there, the jeweler could (1) switch stones when you leave, pulling your diamonds and replacing them with cubic zirconia. When you come back in a week, he tells you, sorry, he couldn't sell your jewelry and maybe you should take it somewhere else. Now he has your diamonds and you have junk jewelry. (2) He could simply lose your merchandise, or (3) he could go out of business, and your jewelry is gone forever. *Never* leave your treasure anywhere! If he wants to keep it, he pays for it. Period.

Warning #2: The Switcheroo—The jeweler makes you an offer, but says he wants to pull the stones from the settings first to get a better look. If he wants to pull the stones, *tell him to do it in front of you!* Keep your eyes on your jewelry at all times. A dishonest jeweler will take your goods into the back room, pull your valuable diamonds, and leave you with junk in a matter of minutes. The jeweler may seem very honest, and he may be very persuasive, but be firm. An honest jeweler will not object to having you watch while he pulls the stones.

Wizard #2: Wholesalers and Diamond Dealer's Clubs

These are found in every major city. They supply local jewelry stores with their diamonds. If you sell to a wholesaler or a dealer's club, expect to get a little less than you would from a jewelry store. They may offer you 2 to 5% below dump. On the other hand, they usually have more money than a struggling jeweler whose assets are tied up in inventory, so if you're looking for a quick sale, you might find one of these wizards in the Yellow Pages under "Diamonds—Wholesale" and head straight for him.

Wizard #3: The Pawnbroker

This is *not* my favorite place to sell jewelry, but it can be an option. It's a good idea to call ahead and make an appointment. While you have the broker on the phone, tell him what you've got and tell him what you expect to get for dump value. If the pawnbroker isn't interested, you'll save yourself a trip.

Generally, pawn shops are not a good option for you. They're used to buying stuff from desperate customers at 10% of wholesale, so more than likely they won't pay what you're asking.

Note: While pawn shops are usually lousy places to *sell* to, they can be great places to *buy* from. This will be discussed later in the book.

Final Review

Our first journey is over. You've learned the Treasure Hunt, the Sherlock Holmes, and "Doing the Donald." You've converted your jewelry into portraits of "Great Dead Americans." And if you didn't understand what I just said, you shouldn't have skipped ahead, you rascal! Go back and read the first three steps and you'll catch up with the class.

Our goal in Section I was to learn how to get top dollar for our own jewelry, for our family's jewelry, and the jewelry of friends. If you've followed my teachings, you no longer have all the shiny baubles you once had, but you do have more money in your piggy bank, and you're wiser in the ways of the world of diamonds and jewelry. You also have the satisfaction of knowing that you got a fair price and didn't get taken to the cleaners.

What's next? If the basics have you hungry for more, you're ready for Section II. The only way to continue this game is to get more treasure, but this time you have to *buy* the treasure and then *resell* it for a profit. That takes more knowledge, and you'll find it in Section II. Let's go!

The following is a letter I received from a client:

The Surprise
A Story of Sweet Success

Dear Fred,

You played a big role in last Friday night's event, so I wanted to share it with you.

What an incredible evening it was! It's impossible for me to describe all the emotions we felt when I set the diamond ring before Leslie's eyes. All I can say is, it was all I had hoped for and more!

When we were seated at our table at Rainbow Lodge, we were presented (to even my surprise) with a bottle of fine Champagne, compliments of my parents. I had told Leslie a little white lie, telling her we were going to Rainbow Lodge to celebrate my mother's birthday. I even had my mom call Leslie at work Friday afternoon, to tell her she was looking forward to seeing her that evening. So it was a perfect setup. Leslie never suspected a thing.

But when the Champagne arrived, I told Leslie that my folks were not coming and that this was actually an early birthday present for her. Again, she fell for it. Then came the big moment!

I filled our Champagne glasses, and took out a poem I had written for Leslie, and handed it to her to read. It was about our wonderful relationship, and she smiled happily as she read it. But I had left off the final two lines, which I recited to her:

"We've played it well, this game of life,
And now I ask: Please be my wife."

With that, I opened the little box I'd held in my lap and set that beautiful ring down in front of her. Fred, it was an indescribable moment. In fact, everything was indescribable to Leslie at that point—when she saw that stunning ring you helped me select, she developed a case of that peculiar ailment, "sudden mouth paralysis." In fact, I had to ask her again if she'd marry me. What a night!

Fred, I can't begin to tell you how much I appreciated your help in choosing that ring. I'll admit I had not looked forward to the process of visiting jewelry stores, sorting through catalogues, etc., in search of the perfect ring. But your knowledge, professionalism, positive attitude, and no-pressure sales approach made it a very pleasant experience. I think I'll write to the *New England Journal of Medicine*, suggesting they name Leslie's form of speechlessness "Cuellar Surprise Syndrome" in your honor.

Again, my deepest and most sincere thanks. And it goes without saying, but I'll say it anyway: I will be back!

Sincerely,
John Alger

PS: Leslie has almost recovered from her case of "Cuellar Surprise Syndrome" and can now speak in complete sentences!

That's truly the greatest part of this business: Making people happy.

Section II

The Part-Timer

THE TREASURE HUNT FOR PART-TIMERS

If you've followed my gems of advice and pearls of wisdom in Section I, you may be a little wealthier and wiser. You learned how to sell jewelry for no less than its dump value. Now we're going to step up to the next level, which could make you wiser still, and quite a bit wealthier. In this section you are going to learn how to *buy diamonds below dump value for resale.* Got that? This is *very important stuff!* We're no longer trying to sell our own treasure, the "family jewels." Now we're moving beyond our own safe deposit boxes and jewelry boxes, and we're going to learn how to acquire jewelry from other people, how to better evaluate it, how to find new wizards to add to our list, and how to increase our profits.

Your first step should be to line up an honest independent appraiser, using the techniques we discussed in Section I. Tell the appraiser you are trying to buy jewelry below dump value to make a little extra money, and you'd like to use his services exclusively if he'll give you a special discount. Find out if he's equipped to pull diamonds out of their settings. In Section I, we didn't want anyone "popping" our diamonds, especially out of our sight. But now we're buying expensive diamonds for resale and we *want* the appraiser to pull them out of their mountings to get the exact weights, the clarity, and the color grades. Besides, a flaw could be hidden beneath a prong, and we want to know about it.

All right, let's begin our Treasure Hunt, in the *Daily News!*

The Classifieds

Every day, 365 days a year, your local newspaper carries classified ads placed by people who are trying to sell jewelry. A lot of those people have no idea what they're doing, have never heard of "dump value," and are just looking for liquidity. They want cash. Some people who place these ads are asking way too much for their jewelry and won't take a nickel less, but many others are looking for quick cash and will take any reasonable offer. That's where we come in. If we can buy their stuff *below* dump value and sell it *at* dump value—we're "Doing the Donald"!

Let's let our fingers do the walking through the classifieds, and I'll show you how to find the "buried treasure." Here's an excerpt from my local paper, the *Houston Chronicle*. Follow along as I go over everything again that we need to do to find treasure in our hometown newspaper:

The Daily News
(Examples from the Trenches)

1038 JEWELRY & GEMS

AAAAAAAAAAAAAAAAAAAAAA
WANT TO SELL YOUR ROLEX?
Absolutely highest cash prices paid
for fine watches, jewelry, dia.
24 hrs buy/sell 713-132-4567

AAAAAAAAAAAAAAAAAAAAAA
★★ CASH BUYERS ★★
Astro City & The Watch Shop
Largest selection of Rolex, Cartier,
diamonds & fine jewelry.
6464 Westheimer

AAA DIAMONDS
5ct - 3ct - 2ct - 1½ ct - 1 ct
Must sell 8am-10pm

ACE WATCH
BUYING & SELLING
ROLEXES, DIAMONDS

A+ Loan or Buy Rolex-Jewelry-car-
truck-tool-most anything
M-F 9-8

ALPHA-PHI-ALPHA
14k gold cufflinks & 14k gold ring.
$200 ea.

API - Absolutely highest $ paid for
all watches. Buy/Sell Diamonds-
Gold-Jewelry

18 Carat yellow gold mid size Piaget
Polo watch, retails $18k, sell $7000

Diamond, 2.05 ct pear, J in color,
SI-2 in clarity, for a fast sell $3,300.
Ser inq only

Diamond ring, ¾ of a carat, SI-2 in
clarity, J in color, appraisal w/
papers $4K. Sell $2500

1038 JEWELRY & GEMS

Diamond ring, purchased Helzberg,
cost $3138, asking $2200. Marquis
ctr stone, 1¾ ct.

Ladies Rolex steel & gold w/ date.
Silver dial. Serviced. Like new.
$1350

Mens Rolex. 18ct & Stainless
Datejust. New in '87. Papers/box
$3000 firm—non nego.

Must sacrifice $6800 engagement
ring. 1ct Solitaire w/baguettes. Sell
for $3800 OBO.

MUST SELL brand new 1 Ct. total
Wt. baguette diamond ring. GIA
appr $2000, will sacrifice $995 obo
will pay for sizing.

MUST SELL!! 14 carat gold ruby &
diamond ring, ⅒ TDW, appraised
value $400, will sacrifice, $199.
Ladies 14 carat necklace, 21 diamonds totaling ⅓ carat, appraised
value $850, will sell for $399.

Rolex Mens & ladies. 2 tone, just
out of pawn. Match pair, $2400 ea.
Jim

Rolex Men's Stainless & Gold GMT
master blk face/blk dial. $2000,
obo.

Rolex Men's Thunderbird SS/gold,
$3000. Rolex Explorer II, 2 mths
old, $2900.

TEXAS WATCH & DIAMOND
ROLEX & DIAMONDS
Buying & Selling

57

Right away I see an ad that catches my eye. It's in the left-hand column, second from the bottom:

> Diamond, 2.05 ct pear, J in color,
> SI-2 in clarity, for a fast sell
> $3,300. Ser inq only

This looks very attractive because the asking price is way below dump value! If we go to the charts we see that the dump value of a 2 ct, J-color, SI-2 is $6,000. If the diamond is what he says, we could make a tidy $2,700 profit on resale. One of two things may be happening here. Either the seller is a fool, and we all know a fool and his money are soon parted, or he's inflating the quality of the stone. People tend to overvalue their own goods; that's human nature. But even if he's inflating the color and clarity by one grade each, we can still make money! The dump value of a 2 ct, I-1, K-color is $4,320, which leaves us a thousand-dollar profit.

The next item that looks tasty is this one:

> AAA DIAMONDS
> 5 ct–3 ct–2 ct–1½ ct–1 ct
> Must sell 8 am–10 pm

What intrigues me is the fact that this guy's obviously got a *lot* of diamonds! This plus the fact that he gives us his business hours leads me to believe he's either in the diamond business or runs a pawn shop. But he hasn't given us any details. We don't know the asking prices or the quality of the diamonds. This is information we'll have to get over the phone. I think this guy's worth a phone call, and if his prices are close to dump value and he's willing to negotiate, it may be time to call the appraiser.

Okay, what else do we find in the ads? A bunch of what I call "dreamers." They are people who have no clue as to what their jewelry is worth and are asking way too much for it. I'll dissect a couple of these ads for you, so you can see why we shouldn't waste our time with them. Here's Dreamer #1:

> Diamond ring, ¾ of a carat, SI-2 in
> clarity, J in color, appraisal w/
> papers $4K. Sell $2500

Dreamer #1 is an idiot if he thinks I'm going to pay $2,500 for that diamond! When we look it up, we find that the dump value is only $1,305—almost half his asking price! This would be a good buy only if it were 10 to 20% *below* dump value, or between $1,044 and $1,174.50. Now here's Dreamer #2:

> Diamond ring, purchased Helzberg,
> cost $3128, asking $2200.
> Marquis
> ctr stone, 1¾ ct

Dreamer #2's ad is a bit confusing but still easy enough to figure out. At first glance, it appears that he's offering a 1¾ ct Marquis diamond for $2,200. But look closer: It says "Marquis *center stone*," which means there are diamonds on either side of it, and he probably means that the total weight of *all* the diamonds is 1¾ ct. When he says the ring *cost* $3,128, we can assume he paid retail for it. We already know that retail is usually double the wholesale cost, so let's deduce that the wholesale price of this ring would be $1,564. We also know that the dump value is 60% of wholesale, and 60% of $1,564 is $938. And he's offering to sell it to us for $2,200??? Dream on!! Finally, we come to Dreamer #3:

> Must sacrifice $6800 engagement ring. 1 ct Solitaire w/baguettes. Sell $3800 OBO.

This dreamer says he has a "$6,800 engagement ring." Notice he didn't say that it *cost* $6,800. So the $6,800 doesn't mean a thing to us, and we can't apply our retail-to-wholesale-to-dump formula. But if we go to the dump value tables and pick an *average quality* 1 ct, SI-1, J-color diamond, we find that its dump value would be $2,640, and our dreamer is asking $1,200 more. The only reason this dreamer might be worth a phone call is that he adds "OBO" ("Or Best Offer"). This means he's willing to negotiate. So what I would do is call him up, get the clarity and color grades, and tell him he's dreaming. But—I would make an offer of 10 to 20% below the dump value and give the guy my phone number. You never know—the dreamer might get desperate, and desperate people do desperate things, like calling you back and accepting your offer!

Okay, you've had a practice run. Now get your own daily paper. Go through the classifieds and copy, clip, or circle every ad that offers diamond jewelry. Now get on the phone and call every seller, and have your dump value tables handy. Ask the following questions:

1. The obvious—Is the jewelry still *available*? If not, next number, please.

2. What *size* are the diamonds? (Carat weight.)

3. Does the seller know the *quality* of the diamonds? (Color grade, clarity grade.)

4. What *shape* are the diamonds? Round diamonds are the most popular and thus a little easier to sell.

5. Does the seller have *lab certificates* for the diamonds? There are three excellent labs in the United States that do independent evaluations of diamonds: European Gem Laboratory (EGL); International Gem Institute (IGI); and the Gemological Institute of America (GIA). Diamonds certified by these labs tend to be more accurately graded than those appraised by a jewelry store.

6. How *old* are the diamonds? Very old diamonds may be what are known as "Old European" or "Old Mine" cuts. In the old days, the diamond cutters tried to get the most weight from the "rough," or uncut stone, and often sacrificed brilliance and sparkle in favor of weight. These cuts are poorly proportioned and are worth less money because they don't get the maximum fire and sparkle out of a diamond.

7. Is the price *negotiable*? As soon as the seller tells you the size and quality of the diamonds, you can look up the dump value while you talk. If the asking price is *above* dump value and *not* negotiable, you don't need to waste any more time. If the price is negotiable, offer the seller 20% below dump value, and be prepared to come up to 15% or even

10% below dump value. Any offer is conditional on the results of an appraisal.

8. After reviewing the seller's data and the dump charts, make a decision. If the diamond is available *below dump*, continue.

- Keep human nature in mind here: As I noted in our dry run through the classified ads, people tend to *overvalue* their merchandise. For example, if the seller says he has a 1 ct, round, SI-2, J-color and he's asking $2,000, we can look at the dump value tables and see that the diamond's dump value is $2,400. Looks like a fast $400 for us, right? But if he's inflating the clarity and color by just one grade, and it's really an I-1, K-color stone, the dump value is only $1,680, and we're going to take a bath if we give him $2,000 for it! That's why our appraiser's role is so important, and that's why we never buy a diamond unless an expert confirms its size and quality.

A Tip From Fred

There tends to be an overabundance of commercial-grade diamonds on the market. Avoid diamonds in the I-1, I-2, and I-3 clarity grades, M or lower in color. The glut of these stones on the market makes them hard to sell even at dump value.

9. *When* is the seller available to see an appraiser? If it looks like a deal might be possible, you'll need to set up an appointment with your appraiser.

10. After you learn the seller's availability, set up an *appointment* with the appraiser.

11. Have the appraiser give you a *stat sheet* (see below) on each piece of jewelry you're thinking of buying.

   • Ask the appraiser to *plot* each diamond. A "plot" is a diagram of the diamond as it appears under the jeweler's loupe, or magnifier, showing each blemish and inclusion. It's like taking a fingerprint of the diamond for later identification.

Example of an Appraiser Stat Sheet

Appraiser Stat Sheet

1. Weight_____

2. Clarity grade_____

3. Color grade_____

4. Is the diamond well-proportioned?
   ❑ Yes   ❑ No

5. Rapaport (wholesale) value_____

6. Plot (see number 11)

- Have the appraiser *pull* every diamond valued at over $1,000 to determine the exact weights and grades.

12. Evaluate the appraiser stat sheets, calculate the dump price, and offer the seller 10 to 20% less. If he accepts—*Voila!* We own new treasure!

Going out of Business

GOB, for short. Here's something else you'll find in the classified ads, or on radio or TV if you keep your eyes and ears open. Or you just may happen to drive by a store with the big red-lettered sign in the window saying, "GOING OUT OF BUSINESS—ALL SALES FINAL."

Anytime we learn of a jewelry store going out of business, it's worth investigating, because guess what? There might be some wonderful treasure in there! There might *not* be, but do you think savvy antique dealers pass up yard sales just because there might *not* be any good stuff? Nine out of ten may have only junk, or good stuff but no bargains. But that tenth one! That's where we strike gold. As I told you earlier, if you expect to make money in this game, expect to put in some hard work. If you love the thrill of the hunt, of making the big score, and you don't mind a little hard work, the rewards can be unlimited.

When you find a GOB jeweler, before you go to the store, try to find out a couple of things:

1. Is he a single, independent store or part of a chain? If he's an "indie," continue—chain stores that are closing one outlet never sell below dump value.

2. When is the last official day he'll be open? You'll always get the best deals during the final days, when the owner's attitude is "Abandon ship!" That's when you're more likely to find new treasure at the right price.

When you first go to the store, try a little trick I call "testing the waters." This will often tell you right away if there are good deals to be had in the store. Here's how it works: Go to the counter where the owner keeps his gold chains. Pick out a basic 14K gold chain and ask him to weigh it, in grams. Thank him very much, and let him go about his business while you make a quiet calculation. Figure out how close his asking price for the gold chain is to its dump price. If the prices are close, this really *is* a GOB sale, and the chances are good that everything in the store is a good deal. But if his price *isn't* close to the dump value, you might as well head for the door.

Fred's Rule of Thumb

A jeweler will almost always price his plain gold jewelry to move first, before he lowers the prices on everything else. By checking a gold price, we find out how low he's willing to go on his merchandise.

65

Assuming that the GOB sale is for real, our next move is to ask to see his loose diamond collection. This is the stuff we can make the most money on. When he pulls out the loose diamonds, be straight with him. Tell him you only want to buy if you can get an unbelievable deal, *below wholesale*, and you only want to see the merchandise that falls into that category. Don't go sorting through the stuff yourself—he knows the inventory better than you do, so take his advice on what the best deals in the store are.

At this point you might be thinking, "Hey, Fred, c'mon! This guy's a jeweler. He must know what dump value is, and he'd never sell below that." To that I say, "The guy's going out of business, right? How smart a jeweler can he be?" True, nine times out of ten you won't find any great deals, but that tenth time the jeweler will let one diamond or pretty bauble slip through his fingers, and it's yours! As I said, this book alone is not a guarantee of easy money. It will only help you to work *smarter*. The only thing that will help you work *harder* is your own motivation. This book plus your effort *will make money*. The harder and smarter you work, the more you'll make.

Look over what the jeweler has to show you. Make notes on the weights, color and clarity grades, and his asking prices. When you leave, you can compare his asking prices with the dump value tables and see if you have a chance of getting any steals. If so, you can head back to the store to negotiate.

Before you leave the store, ask the jeweler if he has any *forfeited jewelry*. That's jewelry a customer put a deposit on and never claimed, or jewelry held on layaway. Some of the best deals can be made on forfeited jewelry.

When you do go back to the store to negotiate, *take your appraiser with you*. Before you put your money down, know for certain what you're paying for. And you're not buying anything unless you're getting it for 10–20% below dump value.

Local and National Auction Houses

Purchasing estate jewelry through auction houses has always been one of my favorite ways to Treasure Hunt. One of the main advantages to a good auction is that in most cases they've done all the Sherlock Holmes stuff for you. All you have to do is ask the right questions and plug the data into your dump value tables. Then you'll know what your *maximum bid* should be on any particular item when it goes on the block. And when I say "maximum bid," my friend, *I mean it!* There's a strange phenomenon that occurs in auctions. It's happened to me— twice—and it can happen to you.

Always go early, to the preview, to makes notes on the items to be auctioned. Each item or group of items—a "lot"— will have a number, and there will be a catalog, often just a photocopied list, describing the items. If the catalog doesn't have all the information you need, seek out the auction people and ask for the pertinent details.

When you register as a bidder, you get a cute little numbered paddle to raise in the air, or at least a numbered cardboard square. Then you take your seat, notes in hand, to wait for your items to come up.

After forty-five minutes of watching the punch bowls, ladderback chairs, and braided rugs come and go, the first item on your wish list is finally on the block. Your heart starts to beat faster as the auctioneer intones, "Lot Number 100, a fine old diamond solitaire, round cut, $1\frac{1}{2}$ carats in a

14K Tiffany setting. Do I have an opening bid of two thousand dollars?"

Immediately you raise your paddle.

"Two thousand from Bidder Number 2. Do I hear twenty-five hundred? Yes, from Bidder Number 3, I have twenty-five hundred. Do I hear three thousand? Yes, three thousand from Bidder Number 1. Do I hear thirty-five hundred?"

You raise your paddle again. This is *mine*, you think. Your eyes gleam, fixated on the treasure held aloft. *Mine!*

"Thirty-five hundred from Bidder Number 2. I have thirty-five hundred. Do I hear four thousand? I repeat, do I hear four thousand?"

Panicked, you raise your paddle again.

"Sorry, Bidder Number 2, you're not allowed to bid against yourself," the auctioneer tells you with a chuckle. Laughter ripples through the crowd as you sink, red-faced, down lower in your chair. In your confusion you forgot that the thirty-five hundred was *your* bid. No matter. It looks like you're going to be high bidder anyway!

"Going once at thirty-five hundred. Going twice at thirty-five hundred . . ."

"Yes! Almost mine," you think, holding your breath.

". . . and I have four thousand in the back, Bidder Number 5. Thank you, and do I hear forty-five hundred?"

That SOB! No one's going to steal *my* treasure! You thrust your paddle into the air aggressively.

"Forty-five hundred, I have forty-five hundred from Bidder Number 2 . . . and five thousand from Bidder Number 5 . . . do I hear fifty-five hundred?"

Yes, dammit! Up goes your paddle again, all reason gone now.

"I have fifty-five hundred from Bidder Number 2. Do I hear six thousand? No? Going once at fifty-five hundred . . . going twice . . . SOLD! To Bidder Number 2 for fifty-five hundred dollars."

The crowd erupts. You've won! You're flushed with the thrill of victory! You're the champ! You showed that two-bit son of a. . . .

And as the next item goes up for bid, you calm down and check your notes. Let's see, I paid $5,500. Hmmm. And the dump value of the piece was . . . OMIGOD! $4,500! I PAID A THOUSAND BUCKS TOO MUCH!

Well, congratulations, ol' buddy. You've just lost your proverbial shirt. You own a piece of jewelry you can't resell without taking a big hit.

Now you're probably thinking, "Fred, you're wasting your breath! I'm too cool, calm, and collected for that *ever* to happen to me! I'm the man!"

Okay, you're the man. But I'm here to tell you, it's happened to *me*—twice! You get caught up in the sheer competition of the bidding, the old testosterone starts coursing through your body, and your brain checks out for a brief vacation while you're in there thumping your chest and making animal sounds. Your inner caveman takes charge. "Ooh ooh ooh! Mine!" And I'll tell you something: Cavemen may have been swell guys and all, but there weren't a lot of caveman millionaires.

I took preventative measures. After my second caveman "victory," I brought a "Bidding Buddy" with me. His orders: Know what my absolute, precalculated top bid should be on any item, and use whatever means necessary short of firearms to stop me from raising that hand if the bidding goes higher. As the wise old lizard says to the young hothead in that great Budweiser TV commercial, "Let it go, Fred."

There are two types of auction houses, local and national. Let's look at them in more detail.

Local Auctions

If you remember only one word I tell you about local auctions, that word should be, "*Beware!*" A lot of local auctions are 24-karat *fakes!* What happens is that a gang of crooks will place ads in the local papers saying, "Government Auction," or "Major Estate Jewelry Auction," or anything else they can think of to get your attention. Then they'll put together a bunch of worthless jewelry with fake appraisals, so that your dumping tables will tell you these are all great deals. They'll put "shills" in the audience—phony bidders who are part of the gang—to keep the bidding going higher. They're experts in knowing when to raise a bid or when to stop and let the sucker make the high bid.

Not *all* of these local auctions are scams—only half of them. If you follow these guidelines you should be okay.

1. Do they accept major credit cards? If they're a cash-and-carry outfit, something's up. This is not to say that because they *do* take credit cards they're legit—but if you use your credit card and later find out that you've been scammed, the credit card company will get your money back.

2. Do they have a money-back guarantee if the jewelry isn't what they claimed it was? If not, you walk.

3. Do they own the jewelry they're auctioning? This is a trick question. Most legitimate auction houses *don't* own the jewelry they sell; they're selling on consignment, and if it doesn't sell they return it to the owner. If the auctioneer says they *do* own the jewelry, the chances are good they're running a scam.

4. Do they give a 1-to-3-day preview of the goods? The crooks give you very little time to preview the merchandise, so there's less chance you'll discover it's fake.

5. Ask for their business card to see if they have a legitimate address or just a P.O. Box. Crooks don't like to be tracked down after they take your money.

National Auction Houses

For every local auction I attend, I attend ten national auctions. The top three are the following:

Christie's
502 Park Avenue
New York, NY 10022-1196
(212) 546-1133

Sotheby's
1334 York Avenue
New York, NY 10021-4806
1-800-444-3709

Phillips Auctioneers
406 E. 79th Street
New York, NY 10021-1402
1-800-825-2781

I recommend calling these auction houses and ordering their catalogs through the mail. Ninety percent of the hard data you'll need to pick the great deals will be in those catalogs. If you want additional information, pick up the phone and call their gemologist. I want to stress that *these auction houses are beyond reproach!* If they tell you a diamond is a 2 ct, VS-1, G, it will *be* a 2 ct, VS-1, G.

I can hear you—you're saying, "Fred, these auction houses are all in New York, and I *ain't!* You think I can just hop on a plane and fly to the Big Apple any time they're running an auction?" Well, guess what, partner, *I* ain't in New York, either, and I "attend" their auctions all the time—by phone! Since you know that what they tell you about their jewelry is solid, and they'll stand behind their merchandise "'til Judgment Day," *you don't have to be there.* Option One is to ask the auction house when you need to call to bid on the items you want and to do your bidding over the phone in real time. Option Two is to tell the auction house, in advance, each piece you're interested in and your top bid for that piece, and then sit back and wait for the auction to end to see what you've gotten. I love doing it this way because I never have to worry about overbidding, and I don't have to make an expensive journey to the auction.

In summary, there you have it—three new ways to acquire treasure: The classified ads, GOB sales, and auction houses. Use them wisely and you'll find lots of new treasure to "Do the Donald" with.

"It's in the Mail"
A Tale of Woe

I'm a big overnight shipping customer, and before I get on with this tale, I want to make it absolutely clear that I don't in any way blame any company for what happened.

That said, I'll begin.

The shipper's man showed up at my office one day, bearing what I knew was a shipment of diamonds. I should explain that because I am a major supplier of diamonds to jewelry stores all across the country, I'm constantly shipping diamonds here, there, and everywhere overnight. And occasionally jewelers will ship diamonds back to me, stones that for one reason or another they didn't use. So I already knew when the delivery man showed up what was in the package.

Well . . . in this case, I knew what *used to be* in the package. What was *supposed* to be in the package. So I signed for it and took it to my office.

There was nothing inside. N-O-T-H-I-N-G. *Nada.* Zip. Zero.

Now, much too late, I examined the package carefully and found the neat razor slit at the very bottom of the thick cardboard envelope where someone had expertly cut the package open, removed the contents, and resealed it with transparent tape.

In a panic, I called the shipper.

"What's up, Fred?" he asked, hearing the urgency in my voice. I told him the package he had sent to me had been tampered with and arrived empty. There was a long pause on the other end of the line.

"Fred, when that package left my hands it contained $50,000 worth of diamonds."

Fifty thousand dollars! Lost because of my carelessness, lost because I *assumed* the package was okay when I signed for it. And because I *did* sign for it, the shipping company was no longer liable and my insurance wouldn't cover the loss. Never *assume*! Examine every package before you sign for it, because your signature on the dotted line means you own it.

To *Assume* makes an *ass* of *u* and *me*.

CHAPTER FIVE

THE
SHERLOCK HOLMES
FOR PART-TIMERS

Still with me, huh? If you've made it this far, I should probably assume you're in to stay and want to know all there is to know about becoming a diamond mogul. So the next step is to improve our diamond education and learn more about the "tools of the trade." Then we'll move on to find new wizards and learn more advanced techniques for "Doing the Donald."

We're going to learn a lot more about carat weight, clarity, and color. We'll learn about "buying shy," which has nothing to do with blushing in the jewelry store. And we'll look at illustrations that will help us judge diamond quality.

Carat Weight in Depth

We already know that a carat is $\frac{1}{5}$ of a gram. But there is a more precise way to measure a diamond's weight. It's called the *point system.* Most diamond weights are given as fractions of a carat, such as $\frac{1}{2}$ ct, $\frac{1}{3}$ ct, and so on. But fractions are only helpful in approximating weight. There are sizes that fall between the common fractions, and in those cases we measure the weight in points. It's very simple: **1 carat = 100 points.** For example, a diamond might weigh 49% of a carat, so its weight would be listed as 49 points. A diamond listed as 2.11 ct is 211 points, or two full carats plus 11 points. It's a nice, clean, precise decimal system for weighing diamonds.

Now I'm going to get you into some other diamond measurements that can be very important to the quality of the diamond. These measurements will also give you a way to calculate the weight of a diamond without pulling it from its setting or without actually putting it on a scale.

You can't just whip out the old tape measure to accurately determine the dimensions of a diamond or any other cut gem without one of the tools of the trade, in this case a *leverage gauge* (more about this tool and where to get it at the end of this chapter). This tool will allow us to get precise measurements, in millimeters, of the diamond's *average diameter* and *depth.* Let's begin with the most common diamond shape, the round cut:

Diagram #1

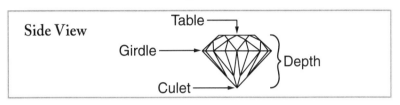

Diagram #2

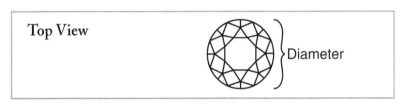

To arrive at the *average diameter,* we'll need to take seven or eight measurements at different points around the girdle, as in Diagram 3:

Diagram #3

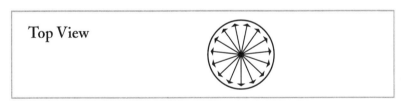

Then take the *high* measurement and the *low* measurement, add them together, and divide by 2:

$$\frac{\text{High + Low}}{2} = \text{Average Diameter}$$

For example, we measure the diamond in Diagram 4, and find that its greatest diameter is 6.5 mm and its smallest diameter is 6.4 mm:

Diagram #4

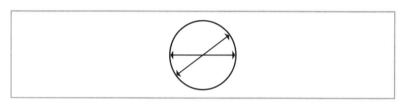

Using the formula above, we calculate the average diameter:

$$\frac{6.5 + 6.4}{2} = \frac{12.9}{2} = 6.45 \text{ mm (\textbf{average diameter})}$$

To find the *depth* of the diamond, measure from the *table* to the *culet* (see Diagram #1). The table is, as you might expect, the flat polished surface on top of the diamond. The culet is the point at the very bottom of the stone.

Once we know the *depth* and the *average diameter* of the diamond, we plug the numbers into this formula:

$$\left(\frac{\text{Average Diameter}}{2}\right)^2 \times \text{Depth} \times .0245 = \textbf{Estimated Weight}$$

For example, we're looking at a round diamond with an *average diameter* of 6.5 mm, and a *depth* of 3.9 mm. Using our formula:

$$\left(\frac{6.5}{2}\right)^2 \times 3.9 \times .0245 = 1.0092468 \text{ (or \textbf{approximately one carat})}$$

For all *other* shapes of diamonds, such as oval, marquise, emerald cut, and pear, we measure the *length, width,* and *depth* of the stone and plug the numbers into the appropriate formula:

Marquise

(Length less ⅓ of width) × width × depth × .0077 =
Diamond's Weight

Example: Length = 10 mm; Width = 5 mm; Depth = 3 mm

(10 − (5 × .33)) × 5 × 3 × .0077 = (diamond weight)
or .964425 or .96 carat or 96% of 1 carat.

Emerald Cut

(Length less ⅓ of width) × width × depth × .013 =
Diamond's Weight

Example: Length = 7 mm; Width = 5 mm; Depth = 3 mm

(7 − (5 × .33)) × 5 × 3 × .013 = (diamond weight) or
1.04325 or 1 full carat and 4 points or 4% of another carat.

Pear Shape

Length × width × depth × .0062 = Diamond's Weight

Example: Length = 7 mm; Width = 5.2 mm; Depth = 3.4 mm

7 × 5.2 × 3.4 × .0062 = .7673 or .76 ct or 76% of 1 carat.

Oval Shape

Diameter squared × depth × .0065 = weight
(to determine diameter, take length + width ÷ 2)

Example: Length = 8.2 mm; Width = 6 mm; Depth = 3.5 mm

First determine diameter: $\dfrac{8.2 + 6}{2}$ = Diameter or 7.1 mm

(7.1 mm) squared × 3.5 mm × .0065 = weight or 1.1468275 or 1 carat and 14 points or 14% of another carat.

Of course, if you own a diamond scale, you won't need these formulas unless the stone is mounted in a setting and you can't pull it and weigh it by itself.

Note: If you're trying to take the measurements of a mounted stone, and the setting prevents you from measuring the depth, I have a little trick which works just as well. The *depth* of a diamond is usually 60% of its maximum diameter or width. So find the average diameter or the width, and simply multiply it by .60. That will give you a fairly accurate estimate of the depth. For example: we have a pear-shaped diamond in a setting, and we can measure the length (9 mm) and the width (6 mm), but we can't get at the bottom of the stone to measure the depth. Just multiply the width (6 mm) by .60 to find the depth:

6 mm × .60 = 3.6 mm

Now we can plug that information into our formula for pear-shaped diamonds to find the approximate weight:

9 × 6 × 3.6 × .0062 = 1.2 ct

Shy Diamonds

This is a term I coined for *undercarated diamonds*. What do I mean by this? Well, when a diamond reaches a full-carat or half-carat weight plateau, the price goes up dramatically. In my first book, *How to Buy a Diamond*,[1] I wrote that it's always smarter to buy "shy"—just below the full-carat and half-carat plateaus. That is, instead of buying a 1 ct diamond, buy a .90 ct diamond, a 90-pointer. Instead of buying a 1 and ½ ct, buying shy would mean buying a 1.49 ct diamond. The reason I recommend shy diamonds is that they *look* the same and they cost less, anywhere from 10% to 30% less than the full-carated or half-carated stones. And it's important for us to know that shy diamonds are worth less, because otherwise we might assign the wrong dump value to a diamond we're thinking of buying.

For example, the dump value of a 1 ct VS-1, G diamond is $3,720, but the dump value of a *shy one-carat diamond,* or a .90 ct stone, is $2,538—a difference of $1,182! (See the *shy diamond dump value tables* that follow.)

If there's a diamond you're thinking of buying, and it's said to be 1 ct or 2 ct, for example, get it onto a scale and make certain. If it's shy, the value goes down considerably.

For all shy diamonds, use the following dump value tables instead of the full-carat and half-carat tables from Section I. I know, I know—another set of tables to deal with. But it's not that complicated, and this is how business is conducted in the wonderful world of diamonds. Just think of them as another tool to help you get rich and to avoid getting cheated. So use the full-carat tables only if the diamond is *no less than*

[1] *How to Buy a Diamond*, Fred Cuellar, Casablanca Press, A Division of Sourcebooks, 1998. ISBN 1-57071-392-8.

the full-carated weight, and use the "shy" charts when the weight is under the full-carated weight. If the diamond is 1.02 ct, use the 1 ct dump value. If it's .99 ct, use the .90 dump value. If the diamond is 2.07 ct, use the 2 ct dump value. If it's 1.91 ct, use the 1.90 dump value.

.49 (SHY ½ CT)

COLOR	IF	VVS-1	VVS-2	VS-1	VS-2	SI-1	SI-2	I-1	I-2	I-3
D	1,646	1,558	1,440	1,176	1,029	852	764	617	470	382
E	1,558	1,499	1,381	1,117	970	823	735	588	470	382
F	1,499	1,381	1,264	1,117	911	793	705	558	441	352
G	1,323	1,205	1,117	940	882	764	676	529	441	352
H	1,058	999	970	823	764	705	617	499	411	352
I	940	882	823	764	675	646	588	470	411	352
J	793	764	705	676	646	588	558	441	411	323
K	705	676	646	588	558	529	499	411	382	323
L	646	617	588	558	529	499	470	382	352	294
M	558	558	529	499	470	441	411	352	323	264

Example: a 0.49 carat, I-2 (clarity), G (color) = $441 dump value.

.69 (SHY ¾ CT)

COLOR	IF	VVS-1	VVS-2	VS-1	VS-2	SI-1	SI-2	I-1	I-2	I-3
D	3,436	2,815	2,566	2,111	1,738	1,490	1,200	952	745	579
E	2,815	2,608	2,235	1,987	1,697	1,449	1,159	910	703	538
F	2,608	2,277	2,028	1,863	1,656	1,366	1,117	869	662	538
G	2,277	2,028	1,890	1,780	1,573	1,283	1,076	828	662	496
H	1,945	1,780	1,614	1,531	1,366	1,242	1,035	786	621	496
I	1,573	1,449	1,366	1,242	1,159	1,076	993	745	621	496
J	1,324	1,242	1,159	1,117	1,076	1,035	952	703	621	455
K	1,076	1,035	993	952	910	869	786	662	579	455
L	1,035	993	952	910	869	828	745	579	538	414
M	869	828	828	786	745	703	662	538	496	372

Example: a .69 carat, SI-2 (clarity), G (color) = $1,076 dump value.

.90 (SHY 1 CT)

COLOR	IF	VVS-1	VVS-2	VS-1	VS-2	SI-1	SI-2	I-1	I-2	I-3
D	4,968	3,888	3,618	3,294	2,862	2,430	1,998	1,620	1,296	864
E	3,942	3,618	3,294	2,916	2,592	2,322	1,998	1,620	1,242	810
F	3,618	3,294	2,862	2,646	2,538	2,268	1,944	1,620	1,188	810
G	3,294	2,862	2,646	2,538	2,430	2,214	1,890	1,566	1,134	756
H	2,862	2,646	2,538	2,430	2,322	2,160	1,836	1,512	1,134	756
I	2,538	2,430	2,322	2,214	2,106	1,998	1,728	1,458	1,080	702
J	2,322	2,268	2,160	2,052	1,944	1,836	1,620	1,404	1,026	702
K	1,980	1,944	1,890	1,782	1,674	1,620	1,404	1,188	972	648
L	1,782	1,566	1,512	1,458	1,404	1,350	1,188	1,080	864	594
M	1,350	1,296	1,296	1,242	1,188	1,134	1,080	1,026	810	594

Example: a .90 carat, I-1 (clarity), J (color) = $1,404 dump value.

1.49 (Shy 1½ ct)

Color	IF	VVS-1	VVS-2	VS-1	VS-2	SI-1	SI-2	I-1	I-2	I-3
D	14,304	9,923	8,418	6,973	5,811	5,095	4,559	3,307	2,324	1,609
E	9,923	8,671	6,973	6,079	5,632	5,006	4,470	3,218	2,324	1,519
F	8,671	7,152	6,168	5,900	5,453	4,917	4,380	3,129	2,235	1,519
G	7,062	6,258	5,811	5,542	5,185	4,827	4,291	3,039	2,145	1,430
H	6,168	5,632	5,364	5,095	4,917	4,648	4,112	2,950	2,056	1,430
I	5,453	5,185	4,917	4,738	4,559	4,291	3,844	2,860	1,966	1,341
J	5,006	4,827	4,648	4,470	4,291	3,933	3,576	2,682	1,877	1,341
K	4,559	4,380	4,291	4,112	3,844	3,665	3,307	2,503	1,788	1,251
L	3,844	3,754	3,665	3,486	3,307	3,129	2,947	2,324	1,698	1,162
M	3,218	3,129	3,039	2,860	2,771	2,503	2,324	1,966	1,609	1,162

Example: a 1.49 carat, VS-1 (clarity), F (color) = $5,900 dump value.

1.90 (Shy 2 ct)

Color	IF	VVS-1	VVS-2	VS-1	VS-2	SI-1	SI-2	I-1	I-2	I-3
D	19,950	13,794	12,540	10,488	8,550	7,296	6,612	4,674	3,306	2,166
E	13,974	12,654	10,602	8,892	8,208	7,182	6,270	4,560	3,306	2,052
F	12,654	10,830	9,234	8,436	7,866	7,068	6,156	4,446	3,192	2,052
G	10,716	9,234	8,322	7,980	7,410	6,840	6,042	4,332	3,078	1,938
H	9,120	8,094	7,638	7,410	7,068	6,726	5,814	4,218	2,964	1,938
I	7,752	7,410	7,068	6,840	6,498	6,042	5,472	4,104	2,850	1,824
J	7,182	6,954	6,612	6,498	5,928	5,700	5,130	3,876	2,736	1,824
K	6,498	6,270	6,042	5,814	5,472	5,130	4,674	3,534	2,622	1,710
L	5,472	5,244	5,130	4,902	4,674	4,446	4,104	3,306	2,508	1,596
M	4,560	4,446	4,332	4,104	3,876	3,534	3,306	2,850	2,280	1,596

Example: a 1.90 carat, VVS-2 (clarity), J (color) = $6,612 dump value.

2.90 (SHY 3 CT)

COLOR	IF	VVS-1	VVS-2	VS-1	VS-2	SI-1	SI-2	I-1	I-2	I-3
D	43,500	33,408	29,058	22,968	18,444	14,268	11,484	7,830	5,394	3,654
E	33,408	29,058	22,968	19,836	16,530	13,920	11,310	7,656	5,394	3,480
F	29,058	23,142	20,532	17,052	15,834	13,572	11,136	7,482	5,394	3,306
G	22,968	20,532	16,878	15,834	14,790	12,876	10,788	7,308	5,220	3,306
H	19,662	16,530	15,312	14,442	13,050	11,832	10,266	7,134	5,046	3,132
I	15,138	14,268	13,746	12,354	11,310	10,614	9,570	6,960	4,872	2,958
J	13,224	12,702	12,006	11,136	10,440	9,744	8,700	6,786	4,698	2,958
K	10,962	10,614	10,266	9,918	9,570	8,874	8,004	6,264	4,524	2,784
L	9,222	8,874	8,526	8,178	7,830	7,482	6,960	5,742	4,350	2,610
M	7,830	7,482	7,134	6,786	6,438	5,916	5,568	4,872	4,002	2,610

Example: a 2.90 carat, SI-1 (clarity), I (color) = $10,614 dump value.

3.90 (SHY 4 CT)

COLOR	IF	VVS-1	VVS-2	VS-1	VS-2	SI-1	SI-2	I-1	I-2	I-3
D	92,430	67,158	56,628	43,758	35,568	29,250	21,762	16,380	10,062	5,616
E	67,158	58,032	43,992	35,568	31,590	27,378	20,358	16,614	9,828	5,382
F	56,628	44,226	35,802	31,590	29,484	25,506	19,422	15,678	9,360	5,148
G	43,758	35,802	31,590	29,484	25,974	22,698	18,252	14,742	9,126	4,914
H	35,568	31,356	28,782	25,974	22,698	19,422	17,082	13,806	8,658	4,914
I	27,846	25,506	24,336	22,464	19,188	17,550	14,976	13,104	8,190	4,680
J	23,166	21,996	21,060	19,188	17,316	15,912	13,806	12,160	7,722	4,446
K	20,592	19,422	18,486	16,848	15,444	14,040	12,168	10,764	7,254	4,212
L	16,146	15,444	14,742	14,040	12,870	11,466	9,828	9,126	6,786	3,978
M	13,104	12,636	12,168	11,700	11,232	10,062	8,658	8,190	6,318	3,978

Example: a 3.90 carat, VVS-1 (clarity), H (color) = $31,356 dump value.

4.90 (SHY 5 CT)

COLOR	IF	VVS-1	VVS-2	VS-1	VS-2	SI-1	SI-2	I-1	I-2	I-3
D	122,010	90,258	77,028	59,388	49,098	40,572	29,400	22,344	12,642	7,056
E	90,258	77,028	59,388	49,098	44,100	37,632	27,930	20,874	12,348	6,762
F	77,028	59,682	49,392	43,218	40,278	34,692	26,754	19,698	11,760	6,468
G	59,388	49,392	43,512	40,278	34,986	30,282	25,572	18,522	11,466	6,174
H	47,628	43,218	38,808	34,986	30,576	27,342	23,520	17,346	10,878	6,174
I	37,338	34,398	62,046	30,576	28,224	24,402	21,756	16,464	10,290	5,880
J	29,988	28,518	27,048	25,518	24,108	21,462	19,698	15,288	9,702	5,586
K	26,460	24,990	23,814	22,050	20,580	18,522	17,052	13,524	9,114	5,292
L	21,168	19,992	19,404	18,522	17,346	15,582	13,818	11,466	8,526	4,998
M	17,640	16,758	16,440	15,816	15,288	13,818	12,348	10,290	7,338	4,998

Example: a 4.90 carat, IF (clarity), D (color) = $122,010 dump value.

Clarity in Depth

The following summary from *How to Buy a Diamond*[2] will give you a deeper understanding of what makes a diamond a specific clarity grade and will teach you how to "spot-grade" a diamond.

The clarity grade of a diamond depends on how clear or "clean" it is—how free it is of blemishes and inclusions, when viewed under the naked eye and with a 10X (ten-power) loupe or magnifier. Let's define our terms:

[2]Summary from Chapter One, *How to Buy a Diamond*, pages 6–19. Fred Cuellar, Casablanca Press, A Division of Sourcebooks, 1998. ISBN 1-57071-392-8.

Blemishes—Imperfections on the outside of a diamond:

Chip	A little piece missing, caused by wear or the cutting process.
Scratch	A line or abrasion on the diamond.
Fracture	A crack on the diamond's surface.
Polishing Lines	Fine lines on the stone's surface formed during the polishing stage.
Natural	An unpolished area of the diamond's surface.
Extra Facets	Additional polished surfaces which should not be there, and which spoil the symmetry of the diamond.
Bearding	Very small fractures on an edge of the diamond.

Inclusions—Imperfections inside a diamond:

Carbon	Black spots inside a stone.
Feather	An internal crack.
Crystal	White spot inside a stone.
Pinpoint	Tiny spot, smaller than a crystal.
Cloud	A group or cluster of pinpoints, which may look like a single, large inclusion.

Loupe (pronounced "loop")—A small magnifying glass used by all jewelers to view gemstones. Any good jeweler or appraiser will let you use one and will show you how. The loupe should be 10X, or ten-power magnification, and the housing around the lens should be black so as not to distort the color of the stone. The Federal Trade Commission requires that diamond grading be done with a 10X loupe, and any flaw that can't be seen under that magnification is considered nonexistent.

Following are the clarity grades for diamonds, as established by the Gemological Society of America (GIA):

Flawless — Free from inclusions and blemishes when viewed under 10X magnification. *Very rare and very expensive.*

Internally flawless — Free from inclusions; may have slight blemishes when viewed under 10X magnification. *Also very rare and very expensive.*

VVS-1 and VVS-2 — Very, very slightly included. Has minute inclusions or blemishes the size of a pinpoint when viewed under 10X magnification. *Rare and expensive.*

VS-1 and VS-2 — Very slightly included. Has inclusions and blemishes smaller than a grain of salt when viewed under 10X magnification. No carbon, no fractures. *High quality.*

SI-1 — Slightly included. Has inclusions or blemishes larger than a grain of salt when viewed under 10X magnification, and these inclusions may be carbon or fractures. Almost all SI-1 diamonds are "eye clean," which means the flaws can't be seen with the naked eye. *Good quality.*

SI-2

Slightly included. Has inclusions or blemishes larger than a grain of salt when viewed under 10X magnification, and some of these flaws may be visible to the naked eye. *Borderline diamond.*

I-1

Imperfect. Has inclusions and blemishes visible to the naked eye. *Commercial grade.*

I-2

Imperfect. Has inclusions and blemishes visible to the naked eye that can make as much as $1/4$ of the diamond appear cloudy and lifeless. *Commercial grade.*

I-3

Imperfect. Has many, many inclusions and blemishes visible to the naked eye, and very little sparkle or fire. Not a pretty diamond. *Bottom of the barrel.*

How to Spot Clarity Grades

Note: All plotting that follows shows what inclusions and blemishes look like in the different clarity grades when viewed under 10X magnification.

In the plotting of the flawless diamond, you will notice there are no marks, meaning that the diamond has no inclusions or blemishes:

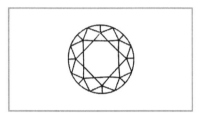

Diagram 1: Flawless

In the plotting of the internally flawless diamond, there are no inclusions. But you will notice the slight markings representing slight blemishes:

 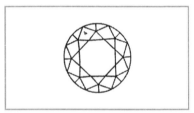

Diagram 2: IF   Diagram 3: IF
(Internally Flawless)   (Internally Flawless)
Scratch   Polishing Lines

In the VVS plottings, you'll see some very minor inclusions and blemishes. *Important Note*: An untrained person will have a very difficult or impossible time trying to find the inclusions or blemishes in a VVS-1 or VVS-2 internally flawless or flawless diamond. Unless you're a gemologist, don't expect to. These top four grades will appear to the average person to be perfectly clean:

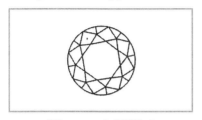

Diagram 4: VVS-1
(Very, Very Slightly Included)
Pinpoint

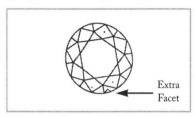

Diagram 5: VVS-1
(Very, Very Slightly Included)
Pinpoints, Extra Facet

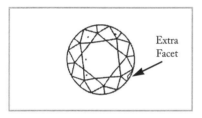

Diagram 6: VVS-1
(Very, Very Slightly Included)
Pinpoints, Extra Facet

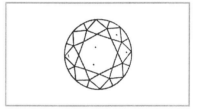

Diagram 7: VVS-1
(Very, Very Slightly Included)
Pinpoints, Scratch, Bearding

In the VS plottings, the pinpoints become a little easier to see. Also, we start to see some of the other types of inclusions and blemishes:

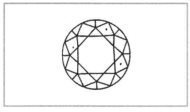

Diagram 8: VS-1
(Very Slightly Included)
Pinpoints

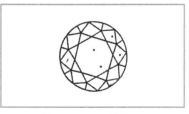

Diagram 9: VS-1
(Very Slightly Included)
Pinpoints, Bearding, Feather

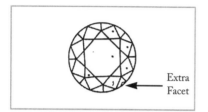

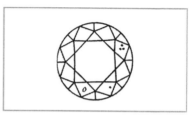

Diagram 10: VS-1
(Very Slightly Included)
Pinpoints, Extra Facets, Feather

Diagram 11: VS-2
(Very Slightly Included)
Pinpoints, Crystal

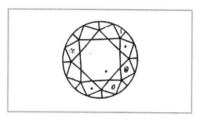

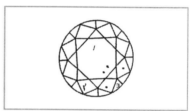

Diagram 12: VS-2
(Very Slightly Included)
Pinpoints, Crystal,
Clouds, Scratch

Diagram 13: VS-2
(Very Slightly Included)
Pinpoints, Crystal,
Feathers, Scratch

In the SI plotting, we start to see larger crystals, pinpoints, feathers, and the introduction of carbon:

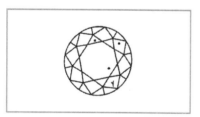

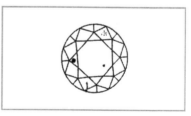

Diagram 14: SI-1
(Slightly Included)
Pinpoints, Feathers

Diagram 15: SI-1
(Slightly Included)
Pinpoints, Carbon,
Feathers, Clouds

Diagram 16: SI-1
(Slightly Included)
Pinpoints, Carbon, Feathers

Diagram 17: SI-2
(Slightly Included)
Carbon, Crystals,
Pinpoints, Feathers

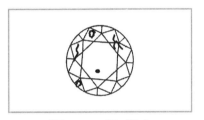

Diagram 18: SI-2
(Slightly Included)
Pinpoints, Carbon, Feather,
Crystals

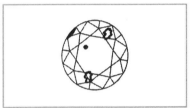

Diagram 19: SI-2
(Slightly Included)
Chip, Carbon, Crystals

In the imperfect plottings, I get an opportunity to really do some drawing! You will see every type of inclusion and blemish in these grades:

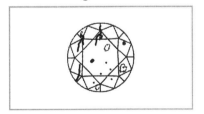

Diagram 20: I-1
(Imperfect)
Feathers, Crystals, Pinpoints

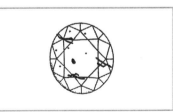

Diagram 21: I-1
(Imperfect)
Carbon, Pinpoints,
Fracture, Bearding

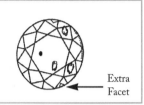

Diagram 22: I-1
(Imperfect)
Carbon, Crystals,
Bearding, Extra Facets

Diagram 23: I-2
(Imperfect)
Carbon, Major Feathers,
Chips, Clouds

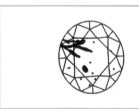

Diagram 24: I-2
(Imperfect)
Pinpoints, Major Feathers,
Carbon, Fractures

Diagram 25: I-2
(Imperfect)
Crystals, Chips,
Clouds, Fractures

Diagram 26: I-3
(Imperfect)
Major Feathers, Bearding,
Crystals, Clouds,
Fracture, Chips

Diagram 27: I-3
(Imperfect)
Chips, Carbon, Major Feathers,
Crystals, Pinpoints

Fake Grade

European Gem Laboratory recently introduced a "nongrade" of diamond. They call it an SI-3. It is only an I-1 diamond with a PR agent! If someone tries to sell you an SI-3, don't be fooled. It's just an imperfect stone.

Color in Depth

The fabulous Hope Diamond, which weighed originally over 112 carats when it first appeared around 1642, has been described as a "beautiful violet" in color. In fact, diamonds come in virtually all colors of the rainbow. But colored diamonds are precious and rare, and the chances are good that all the diamonds you'll find in your treasure hunting will be white or yellow, and the whiter the better. The yellow tint in diamonds comes from their nitrogen content. As a rule, the more yellow the diamond, the less value it has. That's because the yellower it is, the less sharp and sparkly it appears. A whiter stone lets more light pass through it, making it sparkle and shine. The exception to this rule of thumb is the canary diamond, which contains so much nitrogen that it's a brilliant yellow. Canaries, as with all colored diamonds, are called "fancies" and are very rare and very expensive.

The best way to judge the color of a diamond is to compare it with a master set or colorimeter. A master set has been graded in a laboratory. Ask your appraiser to show you his master set, or if you decide you're in the game for good, buy your own set. Compare any diamond you're thinking of buying with the master set to accurately determine the color grade. The second option is to have the color checked using a colorimeter. A colorimeter is a device that grades diamonds and is accurate to within ½ a grade. Using a masterset is only accurate ± one grade.

Fred's Advice—Go for diamonds that are J-color or higher. They are the most beautiful, and therefore the most valuable and easiest to resell. Keep in mind that the *average* diamond sold in the United States is M or N in color, so you'll have to pass on a few dogs before you find a winner.

Commercial Grade Diamonds: A Warning

Commercial-grade diamonds are those with clarity grades I-1, I-2, and I-3 and color grades M or lower. These diamonds are JUNK! I know I've already said this, but it's worth repeating. Bad diamonds don't have a secondary market, they never appreciate in value, and they are totally outside the realm of *Diamonds for Profit*. Big crack, send it back! Yellow like cheese, like a dog with fleas! (Watch for my next book, *The Poetry of Fred Cuellar!*)

Fluorescence—Fluorescence is a diamond's reaction to ultraviolet (UV) light. Some diamonds glow, or *fluoresce,* in different colors under UV light. *This is not a good thing!* The general rule is to avoid diamonds that fluoresce. A diamond that glows strong blue under UV light may look dull in the sunlight. If a diamond you're thinking of buying has strong blue fluorescence, deduct 10% from the price on the dump value table to get its true dump value. For example, if a diamond's dump value is $1,000 but it glows strong blue under UV light, its true dump value is $900. Your honest independent appraiser will have a

---

Quick and Easy Grading Tips

Clarity: 1. If you can see inclusions or blemishes with your own eyes, the diamond is no better than I-1.

2. With a 10X loupe, if you see any black spots, cracks, or anything larger than a grain of salt, the diamond is no better than SI-1.

3. If with a 10X loupe you can see *nothing* wrong with the diamond, it could be a VS-1 or VS-2.

Color: Take a pure white business card and fold it in half. Lay the diamond in the crease. If you pick up *any* yellow, the diamond is no better than a K.

UV light to check for fluorescence, or you can buy a small, portable UV light to check for yourself.

Gembuster
A Tale of Woe

One of the keys to success in this business is having "bench people" who are not only good at what they do, but also people you can trust. Bench people are the men and women behind the scenes in the jewelry business, the skilled artisans who manufacture the jewelry and place the stones in their settings. They're also referred to as stone-setters and goldsmiths.

Finding a good bench person is not easy. The best way to find one is by word of mouth, recommendations from other people in the business. Ask your "dump wizards," the people on the inside of the business, and they'll know who's good and who's not. When you do find one, continue to check his references and background until you're satisfied. And when you're satisfied, get the bench person to sign a contract with you that says he is responsible for diamonds lost or damaged while in his possession. Then, and only then, put the bench person to work for you.

Back in 1986, when my business was growing rapidly, I got careless and hired a bench man without doing a thorough background check and without getting him to sign that contract. It just slipped through the cracks.

"Crack" is an appropriate word at this point in the story. After less than two months on the job, the new bench man cracked one of my diamonds while setting it. When I told him he was liable for the damage, he simply shrugged and walked. No contract, no liability. So in the end, *I* was liable for the loss, $10,000 worth.

God is in the details. So is the Devil. Mind the details.

"DOING THE DONALD" FOR PART-TIMERS

Up to now we have discussed reselling our treasure at dump prices. We've learned about three "wizards" who buy dump diamonds: Jewelry stores, diamond wholesalers and dealers clubs, and pawn shops. In this chapter we are going to meet the biggest buyer of dump diamonds in the United States, and we're going to learn about "brotherly wizards." Selling diamonds to brotherly wizards is what takes us from making merely *good* money to making *buckets* of money and really becoming "The Donald"!

First, let's meet the "Number One Wizard for Dump Diamonds."

The New York Diamond Dealers Club

More diamonds pass through the doors of this club than any other place in the world that I know of. The NYDDC and its members supply wholesale and retail dealers with 80% of all the diamonds sold to end users in the United States. Faced with so much demand, the NYDDC is always a candidate to *buy* diamonds at dump value. And because the club has so many members, you can sometimes get 5% *above dump value* by getting members to bid against each other for your diamond.

There are two major obstacles to this course of action. First, the only way you can sell to the NYDDC is to be a member or to know a member. If you're new to the game, that's two quick strikes against you. I suppose you could hop on a plane to New York and ring doorbells on 47th Street (the heart of New York City's Diamond District) until someone talks to you. Slightly impractical, don't you think? Especially since they'll spot you right away as a "pigeon," a novice, and the NYDDC would never pay dump prices to a pigeon. They'd try to bully you into selling for less.

But don't lose heart. I wouldn't have even brought up these great wizards if I didn't have a way for you to deal with them. Remember, I said the only way to deal with the NYDDC is to be a member or to *know* a member. You know me, and I know lots of members. So I'm offering you the "Fred Connection." Here's the plan, Stan: Any diamonds you can't sell at dump that are SI-1, J or better—CALL ME! That's right, call my Diamonds for Profit Help Line (see page xx and the next page) and someone will help you dump, ship, and get paid. How's that for a deal? I offer this service free, and I ask only one thing: Please don't abuse it. There are folks in rural areas where you just can't dump a diamond who have no option but to use my Help Line. If you live in a metropolitan area which *does* have jewelers, dealers clubs, and pawn shops, try all the local resources before calling me. Then, if for some reason you can't get dump value, call the Help Line. Consider it your safety net, and you're welcome to it. True success in life is determined by how you help other people.

Fred's Help Line:

(713) 222-2728

M–F 9 A.M.–6 P.M. Central Time

Saturday 9 A.M.–12 noon

Brotherly Wizards

Buying diamonds at *below* dump value and selling them *at* dump value is profitable. But I've been noticing the wisps of smoke rising from your ears, which tells me you've been thinking, and I *know* this thought has crept into your mind: "What if I could sell *higher* than dump value? Wouldn't that be . . . y'know . . . BETTER?"

You bet it would be! The big question is, *who* is going to pay more than dump value? Well, let's think this one through. The average person who buys a diamond pays *twice* what he should pay, wholesale × two. (That's called *retail*, in case you've forgotten.) We also know that the average person buys $700 worth of jewelry per year through most of adult life. So . . . before we go off and sell our treasure at dump value, think— Is there someone you know who might be in the market for a birthday, anniversary, Christmas, Hanukkah, or Valentine's Day gift? Someone who would otherwise pay retail, and would be more than happy to buy treasure from you at, say, 20% above dump value? Wouldn't that just make everyone happy, all around? You'd make more money than you would if you sold your treasure at dump, and they *save* money by not paying retail. Isn't this the perfect example of a win-win situation? I think so. "Brotherly wizards." Family and friends who buy your treasure.

To reach these friendly wizards and meet their jewelry needs, you should follow this little "To Do" sheet I've worked up for you. Follow these four steps:

1. Create a mailing list.

2. Create an announcement letter.

3. Create a newsletter.

4. Create gift reminder/wish list service cards.

Let's discuss these in detail.

1. The Mailing List—A good mailing list is a pearl beyond price, believe me. The more information you keep on the list, the more ways you'll be able to use it in marketing your goods and services. Make it as long as you can, as detailed as you can, and constantly update it as new information comes in about anyone on the list. For example, if your cousin Cicely divorces Mortimer and marries Egbert, you don't want to be sending stuff to "Cicely and Mortimer," do you? Or reminding Mortimer that their anniversary is coming up. No, no, no. *Update.*

Start by making a simple list of all the family members and friends you can think of *with whom you'd like to do business.* I add that because we all have family and friends whom we would *not* do business with for one reason or another. ('Nuff said.) Then contact each of these people to fill in any blanks you might have, to create a basic list with the following information:

Mailing List Card

Name: _____

Address: _____

Home phone: _____

Work phone: _____

Cell phone: _____

Pager: _____ Fax: _____

There will be more information to add later, which they will provide you with, such as birthdays, anniversaries, and so forth. (More about that in the "Gift Reminder/Wish List Service Card" section.)

2. Announcement Letters—The main goals of the announcement letter are to (a) let your family and friends know about your new venture and (b) to let them know how your new venture can help them. Tell them you're going into the jewelry business, that you will be acquiring a variety of treasures, and that *they* will have the first crack at buying them from you. Explain that your prices will be way below what they'd pay at the jewelry store, and that it would make

no sense for them to pay retail when they can buy from you for far less. I have found this to be the easiest and fastest way to spread the word to friends and family about your new venture.

If anyone on your mailing list asks how much profit you're going to make, tell them it's none of their . . . wait, strike that! Be honest. Tell them you're charging 10 to 20% above the jewelry's cash liquidity value, to cover the time and effort you've put into the Treasure Hunt and the Sherlock Holmes. I promise you that no one is going to begrudge you that profit, especially when they see how much money they'll save by purchasing jewelry from you. Let's imagine that Sis has her heart set on a pair of diamond stud earrings she's seen in the jewelry store window, which are priced at $2,000. If that store has done the normal retail markup, the *whole-sale* value of the earrings is $1,000, right? And dump value is 60% of that, or $600. You offer the same earrings to her for 20% above dump value, $720, and you're gonna be her favorite brother for *life*. And you've made $120, plus whatever amount *below* dump you managed to buy the earrings for. Winners all around!

In your announcement letter, mention that you'll be sending them "gift reminders" and will be actively treasure hunting to fulfill their personal "wish lists."

Remember to keep your announcement letter positive, upbeat, friendly, direct, and to the point. If you are using a computer, it's easy enough to add a personal note at the beginning. The rest can be all "boilerplate," or the same for every recipient. Here's an example you can use as a guideline:

Sample Announcement Letter

Special Announcement

Dear _____,

How's life on the chicken farm? I hope you and Clarabelle and the kids are having a good summer. [Personal opening, obviously!]

I'm writing to tell you about a new venture I've embarked on, one that could prove to be pretty exciting for both of us. I'm in the jewelry business, and this means I'll be able to offer you some amazingly low prices on jewelry.

How did I get into this business? Well, I picked up a great little book called *Diamonds for Profit.* I learned how to buy diamonds way below wholesale and then resell them at a profit. You see, I learned that a lot of people unknowingly sell jewelry below its true value. I learned how to find those people, buy their jewelry, and resell it at a profit.

But before I sell this jewelry on the secondary market, I've decided to offer it first to my family and friends. I've enclosed my *newsletter*, which lists all the items I've purchased along with their retail values and the prices at which I can sell them to you. You'll see the prices are pretty amazing. By the way, I've had each piece independently appraised so that you'll know you're getting good merchandise.

I've also enclosed a *Gift Reminder and Wish List* card, which I'd like you to fill out. If you have an important gift-giving date coming up, I'll call you to see if I have any treasures which might fill your needs. I'll also keep an eye out for items on your *wish list* and call you if I acquire any of them.

I'll get in touch with you in a few days to get the info on your *Gift Reminder and W ish List* card. And call me any time if you want to know more.

Sincerely (Love) (Best always) (Yours truly),

3. Newsletter—This doesn't have to be a fancy piece of work. Its function is simply to let your brotherly wizards know what treasures you have in your inventory, each one's retail value, the selling price, and the date you acquired it. The date of acquisition is really for you, not them, to remind yourself when you bought a particular piece. If you've had it for two to three months, and none of the brotherly wizards has picked it up, it may be time to settle for dump value.

You decide how often to send out the newsletter, based on how much treasure you're acquiring, and how quickly.

Here's what a sample newsletter might look like:

Sample Newsletter

Fred's Virtual Jewelry Store

Dear Friends and Family,

Here's the latest list of fine jewelry I've acquired. As always, you get the first opportunity to purchase it at below-wholesale prices:

	ITEM	APPRAISED VALUE (Wholesale × 2)	YOUR PRICE	DATE ACQUIRED
1	3 CTW VS-1, H DIAMOND TENNIS BRACELET	$6,000	$2,160	07/02
2	ONE-HALF CT SI-1, H DIAMOND	$3,000	$1,080	07/01
3	1 CTW SI-1, H STUD EARRINGS	$6,000	$2,160	07/01
4	2 CTW SI-1, H ANNIVERSARY BAND	$12,000	$4,320	06/28

If any of these items interest you, please give me a call. I'll keep them in my inventory for two months before selling them on the secondary market.

Best to all!

Fred

4. Gift Reminder/Wish List Service Card—This is a 3 × 5 or 5 × 7 index card that lists each brotherly wizard's name, address, and phone numbers *plus* important dates that he or she considers gift-giving occasions, and the personal wish list of items he or she'd like to acquire someday. Mail one of these to each BW. The brotherly wizards can either fill them out and hang on to them as their own reminder, or mail them back to you. If they keep the card, call them and get the info over the phone so you can keep an identical card in your files. Knowing what's on your BWs' wish lists, you can always keep your eyes open for those items and acquire them when you can. Make a wish come true at 20% above dump, and you'll be a hero!

Also, leave some space on the card to write notes of your conversations with the individual that might later help you sell that person a piece of jewelry.

If index cards are too low-tech for you, there are also computer programs with which you can create customized mailing lists and databases of your clients. These programs will alert you to important dates coming up, such as a client's birthday or anniversary, and even print the mailing labels for your newsletters.

Here's the information that you should have on the front of each card:

Gift Reminder/Wish List Service Card (front)

Name: _____

Address: _____

Home phone: _____ Work phone: _____

Cell phone: _____ Fax: _____ Pager: _____

Wedding anniversary: _____

Other anniversaries (parents, children): _____

Birthdays (Own) (Spouse) (Children)
(Other—Name/Relationship): _____

Gift-giving occasions:

❑ Christmas ❑ Valentine's Day ❑ Hanukkah

❑ Easter ❑ New Year's ❑ Other

Other information: _____

On the back of the card keep the Wish List and a list of contact dates, or the dates of your conversations and the results.

Brotherly Wizard Review

1. Make a list of your potential brotherly wizards.

2. Send an announcement letter to everyone on the list. Personalize each letter.

3. Issue a periodic newsletter, describing your treasures.

4. Fill out Gift Reminder/Wish List cards for each person on your list.

5. Your first mailing should consist of one announcement letter, one Gift Reminder/Wish List card and one newsletter, all in the same envelope, to each person on the list. (If your list is very long, don't mail them all at once because you have to follow up each mailing with a phone call. Don't bite off more than you can chew!)

6. A week after the mailing, call each recipient. Have each person's GR/WL card in front of you when you call, and fill it out during your conversation.

Gift Reminder/Wish List Service Card (back)

Wish List

1. _____ 6. _____
2. _____ 7. _____
3. _____ 8. _____
4. _____ 9. _____
5. _____ 10. _____

Contact Dates

1. _____
2. _____
3. _____
4. _____
5. _____

7. File the cards in a box that has daily and monthly dividers. File the card in the appropriate date compartment, two weeks before the *next important date on the card*. So, if the next important date for a person is his wedding anniversary on July 11, put his card in the June 27 slot. Come June 27, you pull out all the cards for that day and see who has what important date coming up two weeks down the road. It works! The alternative, as I mentioned, is a computer program that eliminates the cards and stores all of this stuff electronically.

8. Check your file on a daily basis!

9. After each acquisition, check your wish lists to see if you can make anyone's wish come true.

10. Every two to four weeks, mail out an updated newsletter to everyone, letting them know what's in your "treasure chest."

Section II Review

Okay, Part-Timer, let's see what we've learned. In Chapter 4, we learned how to acquire new treasure through the classified ads, GOBs (Going Out of Business sales), and local and national auction houses. In Chapter 5, we learned more about the color, clarity, and carat weight of diamonds. We also learned about "shy" diamonds and their dump values. And in Chapter 6, we learned about the best place to sell diamonds at dump in the United States—New York City's Diamond Dealers Club—and how we can make our treasure a lot more profitable by helping our own family and friends, our brotherly wizards.

We also learned that there is no free ride to "Donald Land," but that your extra effort means extra money at the end of the day, and hopefully, more fun along the way.

If I still haven't dumped enough on your plate, and you're still hungry for more, I've got more for you in Section III: The Major Leagues! In Chapters 7, 8, and 9, we'll go into the most advanced Treasure Hunt methods, and go even further with your diamond education, learning how to tell a well-proportioned stone from a poorly proportioned one. And you'll finally meet the "ultimate wizards," who will pay more for your treasure than regular wizards and brotherly wizards combined!

Warning!

The advanced techniques in Section III are not for the dilettante or the dabbler. But if your heart and soul are pure and you're seeking a total transformation of your life, read on!

If you're ready for that, let's head for the Major Leagues!

Off the Cuff
A Story of Sweet Success

"Come on, you gotta be kidding me," I thought. "Five thousand bucks for a pair of cuff links?"

I was doing my regular Sunday morning routine, poring over the classified ads under "Diamonds, Jewelry, Watches," hunting for possible new treasure. But this ad, I thought, was definitely placed by a Dreamer:

Men's diamond cuff links
$5,000.00 the pair
Call (123) 456-7890

Nonetheless, it was the only new ad that had appeared all week. So naturally I called the number, figuring all I had to lose was a little time.

The woman who answered told me each cuff link had a single diamond, but she didn't know how big they were or what quality the stones were.

"Then how did you come up with the $5,000.00 price tag?" I asked.

"Well," she said, "because that's what grand-daddy paid for them fifty years ago. I have the original sales receipt. All I want is to get back what he paid for them."

Fifty years ago! My mind began to race through the numbers. If grand-daddy paid five grand fifty years ago, today they must be worth . . . ? I told her I'd be right over.

Arriving at the address, I introduced myself and the lady ushered me into her living room. She handed me the old original box, with the cuff links inside. I took out my loupe and did a quick (and silent) appraisal.

Each gold cuff link held a 2½ ct, VVS-1, E color diamond. Each of the stones was worth $37,500! I paid her the $5,000.00, thanked her very much, and was on my way.

I *think* my feet touched the ground once or twice as I walked back to my car, but I couldn't swear to it.

Give people what they want,
and sometimes you'll both be happy.

SECTION III

THE MAJOR LEAGUES

WARNING!

Stop!

The first two sections of this book required very little outlay of your own money. Becoming a Major Leaguer, which means going into business for yourself, will require $5,000–$10,000 start-up capital. If you don't have it, work as a Part-Timer until you earn the capital.

Welcome to the Major Leagues! Before you continue, you must swear to me that (1) you have not skipped ahead and that you have read and understand Sections I and II; and that (2) you are committed to *Diamonds for Profit* 100%. This doesn't mean once in a while or whenever you feel like it. This means you're willing to go to the wall and put everything you've got into the business of buying and selling diamonds, and everything you've got into learning these lessons and putting them into practice. If your goal is to make a little "mad money" on the side, and that's all you want from this book, stop right here. You've learned more than enough to make this book very profitable for you. If you are not ready for a new career, and you're not prepared to give this enterprise the necessary hard work and long hours, then turn back now. That's because I'm here to tell you, this is no place for amateurs, and if you *don't* put 100% into these lessons, the techniques won't work and you will fail. Have I scared you? Good. I meant to.

If you're still with me, the following three chapters are *for you!* You're the individual who is already working very hard and getting paid very poorly for your efforts. You're the one who will put the same effort into the diamond business—and I promise you, you will make money—lots of money! Thomas Edison said, "Genius is one-percent inspiration and ninety-nine-percent perspiration." I agree with that, and I'll tell you what: I'll provide the *inspiration* with this book, and if you provide the *perspiration,* you'll make more money than you can spend in two lifetimes. Deal? Let's get on with it.

Laying the Foundation

What we're talking about here is you, going into business for yourself. So before we get into the advanced-level Treasure Hunt, Sherlock Holmes, and "Doing the Donald," I want you to build a foundation for your new business so that you will be able to properly grow and prosper. This foundation consists of a minimum of four basic building blocks:

• Business name

• Business address

• Business cards & stationery

• Answering service

Let's get these blocks in order, one at a time.

Business Name

There are many ways to play the name game. Use your own name, make up a name, whatever. You could give your business a casual image with something like "Diamond Jim," or take a more formal approach, as in "James Brandywine, Fine Diamonds & Gems." Or you could leave your name out of it altogether and go with "Diamonds R Us." (On second thought, maybe not.) Use your home town: "Skunk Hollow Diamond Merchants." Or your home state: "Delaware Diamonds." Or perhaps your favorite river: "Allagash Diamond Traders." Think big: "Diamonds International." Bigger: "Universal Diamonds." You get the idea. The thing to do is make a list of ten, or as many as you can, and run them past your family and friends for opinions. Then pick the *top three* and head for your local courthouse (or the secretary of state's office or other governmental body—a phone call or two will lead you to the right place) to register your business as a *DBA*. This stands for "Doing Business As," and it's the simplest form of business organization. No charter of incorporation or anything like that is necessary—save that for when your business has grown up a little. This simply puts you on record as an entrepreneur who is *doing business as* (your business name here). This little formality can be very important come tax time, when you will need to deduct your legitimate business expenses.

The reason for taking your top three names to the registration place is that your first pick may already be taken, and you'll have to settle for your second choice, or even third.

Business Address

This is the place where you work. If you're thinking of working out of your home, I want to caution you against it. You're going into the diamond business, you're going to be seeing a lot of people you don't know, and you don't need a lot of strangers knowing where you live. I recommend renting an office in an *executive suite.* This is a suite of several independent offices, maybe with other DBAs like you, which share a common lobby or reception area, plus secretarial and telephone service. You can often rent an office in an executive suite for under $500 per month, and sometimes for as low as $250 per month. There are lots of advantages to this. You get a professional receptionist to answer your calls and greet your clients. On a pay-as-you-go basis, you get secretarial services such as typing, copying, and faxing. You can even get a fully furnished office for a small monthly fee. To find one of these places in your town, look in the Yellow Pages under "Executive Suites" or "Office Space Rental."

Once you lease an office, get a telephone line installed. Some office suites may have a phone line for your office already.

Business Cards and Stationery

Time to go to the printer and get business cards, letterhead stationery, and envelopes. This is the basic starter kit. You won't need specialized business forms yet; you can do everything on letterhead. The cards and letterhead should have your business name, your own name, your business telephone and fax numbers, an e-mail address if you're "wired," and your mailing address.

Go to the printer with a budget figure firmly in mind. Printers will always try to talk you into a more expensive package. Keep it simple and stick with the budget.

Answering Service

In this business, communication with clients and potential clients is important. Sometimes you'll need to act quickly so that you don't miss a great deal on a diamond, or miss a sale opportunity.

During business hours you may spend a lot of time out of the office, going to the appraiser's or whatnot, and your secretary/receptionist will handle the incoming phone calls. But *after hours*, when the office is closed, you'll need an answering service so that you don't miss any messages. You'll find answering services in the Yellow Pages—pick one that's been around for a while and has the best rate.

The next step up in communication technology would be to wear a pager, so you can return calls quickly. After that, a cellular phone will ensure that you're never out of reach. Some cellular phone plans have very low monthly rates, but be warned: They're so easy and handy to use that you can run up big monthly bills if you're not careful. The best idea is to not give out your cell phone number but only use it to *make* calls—because you get charged whether it's an incoming or an outgoing call.

Review

1. Do I have a business name?   ☐ Yes   ☐ No

2. Do I have an office?   ☐ Yes   ☐ No

3. Do I have business cards and stationery? ☐ Yes   ☐ No

4. Do I have an answering service?   ☐ Yes   ☐ No

Do not proceed until you've answered "Yes" to all four questions! If you have, let's move on to our "advanced techniques."

CHAPTER SEVEN

THE TREASURE HUNT— ADVANCED LEVEL

Stop!

In Section I and Section II, we learned how to find and make use of an honest independent appraiser who could help us determine the true value of our treasures. This is fine at the One-Timer or Part-Timer levels, but in the Major Leagues it's going to cost us a lot of bucks to keep dragging an appraiser here, there, and everywhere to appraise our stuff. *It's time to become your own appraiser!* Get certified in diamonds. The good news is that you can do this in three to six months through a correspondence course offered by the GIA, the Gemological Institute of America. Call them at 1-800-421-7250 and they'll send you an information booklet, free. Do it.

Now that we're playing in the Major Leagues, we're going to need to find a lot more treasure. In this section, we'll learn about four new ways to find treasure and a new way to finance our business:

- Ad Placements

- Pawning

- Flashcards

- Bulletin Boards

- The DOL Customer

Ad Placements

Remember, in Section II, how we learned to scan the daily newspaper's classified ads to find treasure? What you see in the classifieds is the tip of the iceberg. That's right—for every ad you see in the paper, there are more than a hundred people out there who have jewelry to sell *but are just too lazy to place an ad!* We want to reach those people, and I'll tell you how to do it.

Back on page 57 of this book, the sample classified ads page, we saw this ad at the top of the page:

```
AAAAAAAAAAAAAAAAAAAAAA
WANT TO SELL YOUR ROLEX?
Absolutely highest cash prices paid for
fine watches, jewelry, diamonds.
24 hrs buy/sell   713-132-4567
```

This guy's not selling—he's buying! Why? Because he already knows what you're learning: Diamonds, jewelry, and watches bought at the right price equal *money!* Look in your own newspaper, and I bet you'll find ads placed by people looking to buy diamonds, jewelry, and watches. What the heck, you think, somebody's beaten you to the punch. But don't be discouraged. We have one major advantage over these people: We know what dump value is, and how to get it and sometimes even more. You know who the folks are who run these ads? Ninety-five percent of them are pawnbrokers, and the pawnshop operator cares very little about the exact quality of the diamonds and watches he buys. He has a very basic formula that guarantees him success: *He only pays 10% of wholesale!* That's right—10%! So to have this guy as our competition is no problem. We're going to place our own ad in the paper, and because we're going to offer more money than him, we're going to take his clients, and their treasure will become ours.

Here are some tips on writing and placing an ad.

Placement—Where the ad is on the page makes a difference. We want ours to be the first ad on the page, or at least one of the top three ads, because a lot of people who call to sell jewelry will call only the first two or three for price comparisons. Since most ads are run alphabetically, a smart ad writer will begin with a row of A's to ensure top placement, as the fellow in our example did. The next line needs to list the *items* we're interested in buying. Then give the *hours* the seller can call. Follow that with a *come-on,* or *hook,* describing how well we pay and why. Finally, give our *phone number* or the numbers where we can be reached. Here's a sample:

> **AAAAAAAAAAAAAAAAAAbsolutely**
> The highest price paid for DIAMONDS and JEWELRY! Not a pawn shop. We are a diamond broker and we pay *actual cash liquidation value* for all jewelry! Call 24 hrs, ask for (Your first name).
> Tel: (ac) 456-7890

What makes this a good ad?

1. Instead of just a row of A's, the top line ends in a *word,* giving it some meaning: *Absolutely.*

2. Right up front, we've told the seller our goal: *To buy your jewelry.*

3. We've separated ourselves from the pawnshops, telling the seller we're way above that level: We're *diamond brokers.* None but the desperate want to deal with pawnshops, and even if they *are* desperate, we're offering more money.

4. We've told the seller we will pay *actual cash liquidation value.* The seller won't know what that means, but it sounds impressive and will make our phone ring.

5. We want to make this as easy as possible for the seller, so we've told him he can call us anytime, 24 hours a day.

6. We've given him our first name, so he'll feel more comfortable talking to us.

7. We've given our phone number, so that the seller can reach us.

Caution: Always check your ad carefully the first day it runs. Misprints are common, and if your phone number's wrong by even one digit, you won't get any calls.

After your ad is placed, sit back and take the phone calls. Anyone looking to make a fast buck by selling their jewelry now has a way to reach you. When a caller has something that's interesting to you, "Sherlock Holmes" the merchandise and buy everything that's of good enough quality and priced right. Then haul your new treasure to a wizard and "Do the Donald." Piece of cake!

Pawning

First let's define our terms. *Pawning* is the art of purchasing diamonds, jewelry, and watches from pawnshops for the purpose of resale at a profit. Yes, my friend, "there is gold in them thar hills!" There is enough treasure gathering dust in pawnshops to make thousands of new millionaires. And the reason so little of this treasure is harvested is that, frankly, a lot of people are scared of pawnshops. Be honest—what's your image of pawnshops? Seedy stores in rundown neighborhoods where junkies furtively sell stolen goods for a dime on the dollar? That's the way pawnshops are depicted in the movies, and that's all most people ever see of pawnshops. Truth is, a lot of them are owned by large corporations, are very clean, are in the nicer parts of town, and welcome your business. As I mentioned earlier, pawnbrokers have a formula—they buy at 10% of wholesale. And even though they mark up the goods 100% or 200%, there's still enough room for you to get a good deal, if you do your Sherlock Holmes properly. The key to successful pawning is knowing your stuff, because in most pawnshops, all sales are final. My recommendation: *Pawning is strictly for those of you that have passed the GIA diamond certification course.*

Picking a Pawnshop—The location and ownership of a pawnshop are the most important factors in determining whether a shop is worth your while. What kinds of locations are good? Places with the heaviest traffic. By "traffic" I don't mean the cars that go past the door; I mean the people who most often use pawnshops. For example, let's say there's a military base in your town. A lot of GI's get into financial binds, or experience broken engagements, and they sell their goodies to pawn shops. A pawnshop near that base is probably in a heavy traffic location.

In every major city there's a good side and a bad side of the tracks. Take my advice and stay on the good side—that's where most of the good jewelry is.

What about ownership? Start with the mom and pop shops. In many cases they have no idea what their treasure is worth. The people in the shops owned by major chains tend to be a little sharper, and any good stuff they take in is quickly sent to head-quarters and sold at dump value back to the jewelry industry.

In my experience, someone with the proper training can make $150 an hour pawning just about anywhere in the United States. That's $1,200 for an eight-hour day. Not bad, huh? A lot of work, but it can pay off.

What to Look For—For starters, forget the gold. Pawnshop owners are smart enough to know the dump value of gold, and you'll never be able to buy gold below dump in a pawnshop. Focus on diamonds, the bigger the better. The average size of diamonds sold in the United States is 38 points, or just shy of a half-carat. There's a glut of these small stones on the market. Stay away from them, and look for stones a half-carat or larger. And *don't buy commercial-grade diamonds*. There is no secondary market for diamonds with clarity grades lower than SI-2 or color grades lower than L.

Recruiting—You can't be everywhere at once, which is why I love "pawnshop recruiting." By this I mean building a relationship with the owner or manager of each pawnshop you frequent so that he calls you whenever some great merchandise comes in. I'll usually strike up a conversation and introduce myself as a guy who's out to make a little small change on jewelry.

I'll say something like, "Hi, I'm Fred Cuellar. Nice to meet you. To tell you the truth, I'm on a little scavenger hunt—looking for some nice jewelry I can resell to make a little extra pocket change."

They'll respect that. Don't come on like "Mr. Worldwide Diamond Mogul," or they'll feel like you're trying to take advantage of them, so they'll jack up their prices. Be a humble guy, a small-timer like him. Give the pawnbroker your business card, tell him exactly what you're looking for, and ask him to call you if anything turns up. Drop a hint that if you get a really good deal, there might be something in it for him.

Your goal is to get as many pawnshop owners as possible working for you. And whether or not they call you, visit them regularly to nourish the relationship. Sometimes it takes three or four visits to a shop before you get lucky. Schedule the visits on your calendar and stick to the schedule. The more pawnshops and the more relationships, the more the treasure you'll accumulate—because this is all about treasure, isn't it? Without treasure, there is no joy in Mudville.

Flashcards and Bulletin Boards

Flashcards are business cards that carry only two pieces of information:

Sample Flashcard

CASH

FOR

DIAMONDS

(A/C) YOUR NUMBER

Have thousands of these cards printed up. Don't put your name or address on flashcards. That way people have to talk to you before you let them visit you.

What do you do with these cards? Leave them everywhere. Leave them in restaurant restrooms, scatter them in malls, place them on car windshields, tape them in telephone booths. Leave your flashcard anywhere you can think of, where people will see it.

Bulletin boards are the best places to leave flashcards. Supermarkets, coffee shops, school dorms, campus buildings, nightclubs, anywhere that has a bulletin board, your flashcard should be there. My personal goal is to distribute a thousand flashcards *per week!* I have found that the response rate is one-half of one percent, which means that for every thousand cards I put out there, I get five calls from people who want to sell their treasure. Five out of a thousand? But Fred, isn't that a lot of work for only a small payoff? Well, I average $500 profit from every flashcard response. 5 × $500 = $2,500 per week, $10,000 per month, just for laying down a few flashcards everywhere I go. Now do you think it's worth it?

If you're still not convinced, let me tell you a little story. A true story. About two years ago, I got a call from an elderly woman who told me she'd seen my flashcard pinned to a bulletin board outside a Kroger's. She told me she had inherited her mother's engagement ring and wanted to sell it. Of course, I set up an appointment to meet her. She showed up with a marquise diamond, about ¾ carat. It was a VS-1, a very nice stone, but the color was blue-gray. Now, fancy-colored diamonds are very rare and valuable *if they're natural*. The problem is that a lot of fancy colors are created by irradiating or otherwise treating the stone, and if the color is man-made, the diamond is worth hardly anything. And the only way to tell for sure is to send the stone to the GIA lab for examination.

I told the lady that since I couldn't tell if the blue-gray color was natural, I'd have to value it as a treated stone, at $1,700. But if she'd let me get the diamond checked to see if the color was natural, it might be worth a whole lot more. She refused! She said she was happy to take the $1,700. I asked her to leave her phone number so that if the diamond turned out to be a natural, I could call her. Again she refused! She told me she never wanted anything to do with that diamond once she left my office. I asked why, and she told me the story.

"This was the ring my father had proposed with," she began. "When I was still a young child, my father passed away.

After a couple of years, my mother remarried, and her second husband was not a wealthy man. He couldn't afford to give my mother a new diamond, so she continued to wear this one. My mother and stepfather argued a lot, and whenever they did, she would wave this ring in his face and tell him he was a loser who couldn't even buy her a diamond, and thank God for her first husband or she'd have no ring at all."

As the old lady continued with her story, I could see tears welling up in her eyes as she remembered her mother's cruel treatment of her poor husband.

"I spent my life watching that woman use this ring as a dagger to the heart of the only father I ever really knew. When my mother passed away recently, I discovered a little note tucked into the bottom of the box where the ring was kept. It said, 'Property of Betty Faron, 1/15/29.' That was me! My father had left this ring to me, not to my mother, when he passed away, but my mother hid this from me all her life so that the ring would never leave her finger."

I understood then why this lady felt as she did toward the ring. I paid her $1,700, and she left with a smile, as though a great weight had been lifted from her shoulders.

The ring went to the GIA lab for evaluation. It was a natural blue-gray stone, and I sold it six months later for $24,000.

Yes, my friend, flashcards can pay.

The DOL Customer

I'd like you to pay very close attention to this section. Do you remember why I always refer to Step Three, selling your treasure for a profit, as "Doing the Donald"? That phrase refers to Donald Trump, who has an absolute genius for getting rich using other people's money. That's what we're going to talk about right now—doing the things I'm teaching you *without putting your own money on the line.* That's right—buy treasure with someone else's money! Sound incredible? Read on.

If by now you haven't raised the question, "Hey, Fred, where am I supposed to get all this cold hard cash to buy all this treasure I find"? you probably have enough money *without* going into the diamond business. I've left this gem of tradecraft until now because, frankly, it's of no use to One-Timers and too big a gun for Part-Timers. This is FYEO—For Your Eyes Only, my Big Leaguers!

A drum roll, please . . . announcing *the DOL (Deal of a Lifetime) customer!*

Here's the way it works. Approach any family members or close friends you trust and ask them if they would be interested in doing two things: First, helping you out, and second, making money in the process. They may not be all *that* interested in the first one until you combine it with the second one, making money.

Explain to these potential bankrollers that until your business generates some cash flow, you need a few DOL customers to help buy the treasure. The reason I call them "Deal of a Lifetime" customers is that you're going to offer them a 10% return on their money within 90 days! Where else can they get that kind of deal? You explain to them that because you only *buy* jewelry at 10 to 20% below its cash liquidity value, or dump value, and because you can always *sell* it for dump value, their money is never at risk, and they'll get their original investment back plus 10%, regardless of what *you* make on the jewelry.

At this point the DOL will reach for his checkbook and ask you how much you need. And you'll explain that you don't need the money until you find a piece of treasure, but when you do, how much can you count on him for?

It's that simple. Your friends and family members make money at a better rate than they'd get on the market, you get your hands on cash for your Treasure Hunt, and I get to feel like a hero when you call me up one day to tell me how much money you've made! What could be sweeter? You may be thinking, "Wait a minute! If I give 10% to the DOL, that leaves less for me." Sure, but half of something is better than all of nothing. Let's look at what happens: Say you find a nice diamond with a dump value of $4,000, and you can buy it for 15% below dump, or $3,400. You borrow the $3,400 from your DOL customer, promising to pay back the $3,400 plus 10%, $340, for a total of $3,740, within 90 days.

You buy the diamond for $3,400. Now you have 90 days to find a brotherly wizard who will pay 20% above dump value, or an ultimate wizard (to be discussed in detail in Chapter 9) who may pay even more, before you're forced to sell it to a dump wizard. The *worst* case scenario is that you're going to make $260 on this diamond. That's selling it at dump, $4,000, minus your DOL's $3,740. If you sell it at 20% *above* dump, $4,800, you're ahead $1,060! And not a nickel of your own money ever left the barn! Is this a great country, or what?

Review

This has been a very important chapter. If you've followed my advice, you're well on your way toward setting up your basic office and getting certified in diamonds by the GIA. We've discussed new ways to acquire treasure: *Ad placement, pawning, flashcards, and bulletin boards.* And, most important, we've learned how to raise cash from "Deal of a Lifetime" customers, because without that cash flow, there's no treasure.

Quick and Easy Pawning Tips

1. To do on-cite "Sherlock Holmes-ing," bring your *leverage gauge*, your *color master set*, and your *10X loupe*.

2. Reject any diamond that has cracks, breaks, or black spots that are visible to your naked eye.

3. Reject any diamond that, when viewed under your loupe, looks like a bomb went off inside it.

4. Reject any diamond that looks yellower than the "L" stone from your master set.

5. Consider for purchase any diamond that you view with your loupe and say, "Wow! This is a clean diamond!"

6. Calculate the weight of each diamond by measuring the width, length, and depth with your leverage gauge. (In a pawnshop, most diamonds will be in settings, so this is the only way to calculate the weight.)

7. If you're looking at a large diamond, one carat or bigger, don't be shy about asking the pawnbroker to pull the stone from its setting so you can weigh it and grade it more carefully. The pawnbroker is usually glad to oblige on an item that large.

8. After determining the weight, clarity grade, and color grade, look up the dump value. Make an offer of 20% below dump value, and if that doesn't work, come up to 15% and finally 10% below dump.

The Perfect Engagement Ring
A Story of Sweet Success

Many years ago when I was just starting out in the diamond business and was watching every penny, I didn't think I could afford to give a customer a break on a price. Hey, I needed every buck I could bring in. That operating principle was put to the test one day when a starry-eyed young couple came in, shopping for an engagement ring.

After looking over what I had to offer, they chose one of the prettiest stones in the lot—too pretty, in fact, for their budget. I watched their faces as they admired the diamond. It was exactly what they were hoping for, and the young woman's face shone with the innocent joy of a child at Christmas.

I played the Grinch. When I told them the price, even though I thought it was a good price and the best I could do on that diamond, their faces fell. The young man whispered into his fiancée's ear, and with a look of great disappointment she reluctantly handed the stone back to me. I knew he had told her the diamond was beyond their means.

That look on her face went straight to my heart, and my heart said, "Fred, make a little less on this one. You'll make it up later somehow."

I held up the stone and made a show of examining it carefully.

"Oh, wait a minute," I said. "I'm sorry. I misquoted the price on this one." I then quoted a substantially lower price, one that I guessed they could afford.

It was like throwing the switch that turns on the National Christmas Tree. The bride-to-be's face lit up with a million-watt smile. I think the young man knew what I had done, but that was our little secret. I wrapped up the ring for them and they practically floated out of the store.

A few days later a letter came from the young woman:

Dear Fred,

I wanted to take a moment to thank you for the time you shared with Brian and me.

I'm in sales, and I work with an extremely wealthy (not to mention critical) circle of clients. What we could afford at retail I would have been embarrassed to wear! But just as much as your prices, I appreciate the patience you showed us. Believe me, I will refer future business to you.

I hope you go to sleep tonight knowing you made a struggling young couple's life a much easier place to be.

Best wishes,
Julianne

I firmly believe that the kindness you show others
will come back to you tenfold.

THE SHERLOCK HOLMES– ADVANCED LEVEL

Okay, Big Leaguers, this is my last chance to lay some education on you. In this chapter we'll go about as far as you can go without getting GIA-certified in diamonds. We'll learn in greater depth about the last of the four C's: *Cut*. We'll study the formulas for determining dump values of big diamonds. And we'll learn about the significance of gem trade laboratories and their role in the diamond industry.

Cut

In this world there are well-proportioned diamonds and there are poorly proportioned diamonds, and we need to be able to tell them apart. To begin, let's look at the parts of a diamond.

The Parts of a Diamond

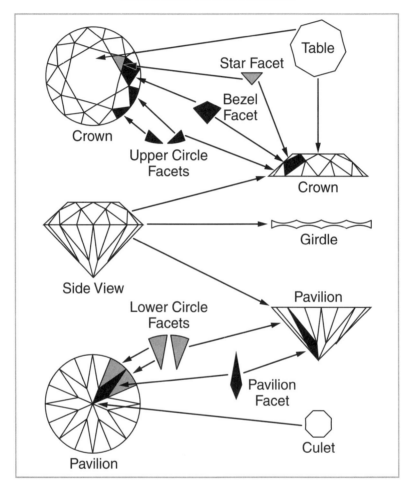

As we see in the diagram, there are three main parts to a diamond: The *crown,* the *girdle,* and the *pavilion.*

The *pavilion,* or bottom part of the diamond, plays a very important role in the appearance of the diamond. The round diamond in our illustration has 58 facets (polished surfaces)—33 on the crown and 25 on the pavilion. The purpose of the crown facets is to catch the white light coming in and to break it up into all of the colors in the spectrum. The pavilion facets reflect it back out through the crown into the beholder's eyes. These reflected colors give the diamond what's called *fire*—the dispersion of the colors of light. The facets of the pavilion also reflect the white light, giving the diamond *brilliance.* The *sparkle* of a diamond is a combination of its *brilliance* plus its *fire.* The better the pavilion performs this function, the better the diamond looks. And the pavilion can't do this job properly unless it's cut well.

Not all diamonds have the same number of facets. *Radiants* and *box radiants* have 75 facets, which tends to produce more fire in their sparkle.

As a rule, the more facets a diamond has, the more it sparkles. Very small diamonds, one-twentieth of a carat and under, are usually cut with 16 or 17 facets. These diamonds are called *single cuts,* and they don't sparkle very much.

American Ideal, or Tolkowsky Cut—In the early 1900s, a brilliant diamond cutter named Marcel Tolkowsky set out to find the perfect dimensions for a diamond. He made adjustments in the depth, the height of the crown, the shape of the pavilion, and the thickness of the girdle until he came up with the proportions that would best refract and reflect the light entering the diamond. His final formula was so efficient that it reflects as much as 92% of the light that enters it, and this came to be known as the "American Ideal Cut," or "Tolkowsky Cut."

The first lesson in measuring a diamond is that the diamond's *diameter* is the basis for all other measurements. For example, if I say that the *table percentage* is 60%, I mean that it is 60% of the diameter. Or if I say the *total depth percentage* is 62%, I mean that it's 62% of the diameter.

To measure the diameter, you'll need to use your leverage gauge:

Measuring the Diameter of a Diamond

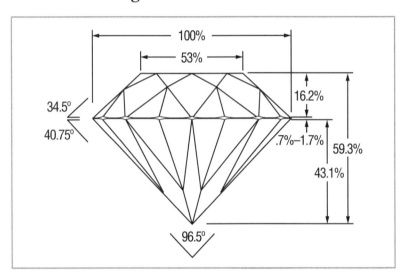

Table Percentage—I've told you that *sparkle = brilliance + fire (dispersion)*. Brilliance is a function of the *table percentage*. The *table* is the largest facet on the diamond, the flat surface at the top of the crown. If the table is too small, the diamond will have very little brilliance. If it's too large, it will have so much brilliance that it will appear hazy or fuzzy. *A well-proportioned stone will have a table percentage of no less than 53% and no greater than 64%.*

To find the table percentage, measure the width of the crown and divide it by the diameter. For example, if the table is 4 mm and the diameter is 6.5 mm, the diamond's table percentage is 4 ÷ 6.5 = .615, or 61.5 percent. This means that this diamond's brilliance will be 61.5% of its sparkle.

Crown Angles and Pavilion Angles—These two angles are the most important angles on the diamond. They determine whether a diamond is top heavy, too deep, too shallow, or just right.

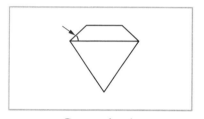

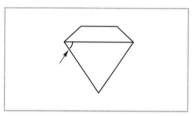

Crown Angle   Pavilion Angle

The *crown angle* determines the crown height. If the crown angle is less than 32 degrees, it makes the table too large. It will look like a skating rink, and it will make the diamond look fuzzy and hazy. A diamond with a flat top and very little crown height is called "spread cut." It makes the diamond appear larger than it really is, but a spread-cut diamond generally returns only 32 to 35% of the light that enters it, versus the 88 to 92% that a well-cut diamond returns.

If the crown angle is greater than 35 degrees the diamond becomes top-heavy. It shrinks the table percentage, diminishing the diamond's brilliance. Also, when the crown is too large it generally reduces the diameter of the stone, making it appear smaller than it really is. *The crown angle should be between 32° and 35°.*

The *pavilion angle* is even more important. Even if the crown angle is not right, if the pavilion angle is correct the diamond

145

will still sparkle well. So if we have to pick one, we'd go with the pavilion angle. The problem is that if the crown angle is off, the chances are that the pavilion angle will be, too. As a rule, if the pavilion angle is right on, the rest of the proportions will fall neatly into place.

If the pavilion angle is *wrong,* the diamond becomes too deep or too shallow and light will leak out through the bottom of the diamond rather than being reflected back into your eyes.

In a round diamond, there can be no "play" in the pavilion angle: *The pavilion angle of a round diamond must be exactly 40.75°.** If it's even a quarter of a degree larger or smaller, it will have a dramatic, negative effect on the diamond's sparkle.

With other shapes, the pavilion angle may vary from 39.25° to 40.75° without affecting the brilliance and fire of the diamond.

For measuring the crown angle and the pavilion angle, I've found nothing better than the proportion scope sold by Gem Instruments. It's fantastic.

Girdle—The girdle is just what you'd expect—that belt around the fattest part of the stone. The sole purpose of the girdle is to protect the edge of the diamond. We look for two factors in evaluating a girdle: How *thick* it is and how it's *finished.*

The finish can be polished, unpolished, or faceted. A polished girdle is smooth, like the rest of the diamond. An unpolished girdle has a frosty look, like a chalk line around the diamond. It's rough, unattractive, and tends to invite nicks and chips.

The best type is the faceted girdle. It has tiny perpendicular facets all the way around. It resists chipping and tends to give off a bit of sparkle from its edges.

---

*based on H.E.M. – human eye measurement

The *thickness* of the girdle is also important, since the primary purpose of the girdle is to protect the stone. Regardless of how it's finished, a girdle that's too thin tends to chip and break more easily. A girdle that's too thick makes the diamond look clunky and unattractive. *The girdle should be .7%–1.7% of the diamond's diameter.*

A poorly proportioned girdle is often a dead giveaway that there's trouble right here in River City. Nine out of ten diamonds I see that have too-thin or too-thick girdles also have poor crown and/or pavilion angles.

Culet—At the base of the pavilion, where the diamond comes to a point, there may be a small facet called a *culet.* If this facet is too large, when you look straight down through the crown it will appear that the diamond has a hole in the bottom. Make sure the stone has no culet or a very small culet.

Total Depth Percentage—Remember, all percentages are based on the diamond's diameter: Total Depth Percentage = (Crown Height + Girdle Thickness + Pavilion Depth) ÷ Diameter.

That is, with your leverage gauge, measure the overall depth of the diamond, from the top of the crown (table) to the bottom of the pavilion (culet). Divide that measurement by the diameter. *A well-proportioned diamond will have a depth percentage between 56% and 61%. For a rectangular diamond, the percentage can be as high as 65%.*

When the percentage is *less* than 56%, it means that the stone is shallow-cut. If it's *more* than 61%, the stone is deep-cut. Either way, it means that either the crown angle is wrong, or the pavilion angle is wrong, or the girdle thickness is off, or a combination of all three factors. And this results in a diamond that doesn't look right and won't give you the maximum sparkle.

Polish and Symmetry—In the cutting of a diamond, once the stone has been cut to certain angles the cutter's final job is to create the final facets and then polish the stone. A lot can go wrong here at the hands of a bad diamond cutter.

If the diamond's basic shape is not uniform—that is, if there is an extra facet, or if the facets are not uniform in size and shape—the stone is said to have poor symmetry. If the diamond is a bit off-round, or lopsided, it has poor symmetry.

If the facets don't have a mirror-like finish, if you can see lines left by the polishing wheel, then the diamond's polish is poor.

Polish and *symmetry* are graded terms—poor, good, very good, and excellent—because their effect on the quality of the diamond is as important as the other factors we've discussed.

Length-to-Width Ratio—A round diamond should be— duh!—*round.* That's a no-brainer, and don't accept a so-called round diamond that's obviously out-of-round. The diameter should be almost exactly the same, no matter where it's measured.

Fancy shapes—that is, all shapes other than round—also have their proper ratios. A marquise shouldn't be so narrow that it looks like a banana or so fat it looks like a football. It just wouldn't *look* right.

Furthermore, if the length-to-width ratio is off, it will intensify the so-called *bow-tie* effect. Every fancy shape has a bow-tie-shaped shadow through the middle of the stone, which can be seen when you look down through the crown. It's caused by light leaking out of the stone, and it's a natural phenomenon in any stone that's not round. But if the length-to-width ratio is off, the bow tie appears bigger, and this is not a good thing because the bigger the shadow, the less sparkle you have.

For a marquise, the proper ratio should be between 1.75 to 1 (minimum) and 2 to 1 (maximum). That is, the diamond should be *at least* 75% longer than it is wide, and *no more than* twice as long as it is wide.

For emerald and oval shapes, the ratios are 1.3 to 1 (minimum) to 1.75 to 1 (maximum). That is, they should be *at least* 30% longer than they are wide and *no more than* 75% longer than wide. For pear shapes, the length should be no less than 1.5 times the width and no more than 1.75 times the width. That is, they should be *at least* 50% longer than they are wide, and *no more than* 75% longer than they are wide.

Proportions Made Easy

The GIA has made it easier to determine if a diamond is well-proportioned by dividing all cut diamonds into four classes: Class One and Class Two diamonds are well-proportioned. Class Three and Class Four diamonds are not (see the diagrams on the following pages). When a diamond is graded Class One, it's like getting an A+ on an exam. A Class One stone is investment-quality, beautifully cut and proportioned, and priced to match. Class Two diamonds get straight A's on the same exam. *Fred's advice: Don't go below Class Two.*

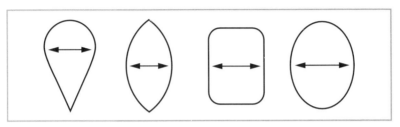

The diameter of any shaped diamond other than round is the diamond's maximum width.

GIA Classes of Cuts*

CLASS I AMERICAN/TOLKOWSKY CUT	
TABLE %	53%–60% OF DIAMETER OF STONE
TOTAL DEPTH	59.3%–61% OF DIAMETER OF STONE
CROWN ANGLE	34–35 DEGREES
CROWN HEIGHT	16.2% OF DIAMETER OF STONE
GIRDLE THICKNESS	.7–1.7% OF DIAMETER OF STONE
PAVILION ANGLE	40.75 DEGREES FOR ROUNDS; 39.25 TO 40.75 DEGREES FOR ALL OTHER SHAPES
PAVILION DEPTH	43.1% OF DIAMETER OF STONE
CLASS II	
TABLE %	53–64%
CROWN ANGLES	32–34.5 DEGREES
GIRDLE THICKNESS	THIN TO THICK (MEDIUM PREFERRED)
PAVILION ANGLE	40.75 DEGREES FOR ROUNDS; 39.25 TO 40.75 DEGREES FOR ALL OTHER SHAPES
POLISH & SYMMETRY	GOOD

*All measurements are calculated by human eye measurement (H.E.M.). That is, the human eye was necessary in the use of reading gauges and millimeter rulers. For more precise measurements the use of a megascope, which is 35 times more accurate than the human eye in measuring proportions, is recommended. The megascope will be discussed at the end of the book.

GIA Classes of Cuts *(CONTINUED)*

CLASS III	
TABLE %	65–70%
CROWN ANGLES	30–32 DEGREES
GIRDLE THICKNESS	VERY THIN OR VERY THICK
PAVILION ANGLE	ANY MEASUREMENT OTHER THAN 40.75 DEGREES FOR ROUNDS OR 39.25 TO 40.75 DEGREES FOR ALL OTHER SHAPES
POLISH & SYMMETRY	FAIR TO GOOD
CLASS IV	
TABLE %	70% AND ABOVE
CROWN ANGLES	30 DEGREES AND BELOW
GIRDLE THICKNESS	VERY THIN OR VERY THICK
PAVILION ANGLE	ANY MEASUREMENT OTHER THAN 40.75 DEGREES FOR ROUNDS OR 39.25 TO 40.75 DEGREES FOR ALL OTHER SHAPES
POLISH & SYMMETRY	FAIR TO POOR

True Dump Value (How Cut Affects Price)

We've seen how the carat weight and the color and clarity grades of diamonds affect their value. Well, the fourth C, *cut*, also has an impact on the price. A poorly proportioned diamond is simply not as valuable as a well-proportioned diamond, all other things being equal. Here's the price adjustment table for all diamonds based on the class of their cut:

PRICE ADJUSTMENT TABLE FOR ALL DIAMONDS BASED ON CLASS OF CUT

CLASS 1	DUMP *PLUS* 43%
CLASS 2	DUMP (PLUS 33%)
CLASS 3	DUMP
CLASS 4	DUMP *MINUS* 15% TO 60%

Let's say we've found a 1 ct, VS-1, J diamond. We go to our tables and find that the general dump value of the stone is $3,000. But to find the diamond's *true* or precise dump value, we have to take its *cut* into account. If the cut is Class 1, the dump value rises by 43%, to $4,290. If it's a Class 2 cut, the dump value rises by 33%, to $3,990. If it's a Class 3, the dump value remains at $3,000. And if it's a Class 4, the dump value falls to between $2,550 to $1,200.

As you can see, the class of cut is very important to the diamond's dump value!

"But Fred! Why didn't you tell me this before?" Frankly, if you're a One-Timer or a Part-Timer, this just isn't going to come into play very often, if ever. The general dump tables will be fine.

But in the Major Leagues, that isn't good enough. One off-make (poorly proportioned) diamond can wipe out the profits from the other nine deals you've made. If you're going to be a pro, and if you're serious about making a career of this business, *approximately* just isn't good enough. You have to know *exactly* what the true dump value of a diamond is, and that means you need to know *exactly* what class of cut it is. Being close only counts in horseshoes and hand grenades.

Buying Big Diamonds

If you're thinking of purchasing a *large* diamond, in the six to ten carat range, here's the formula for determining the dump value:

1. Determine the *clarity* and *color* grades of the diamond.

2. Determine the carat weight.

3. Go to the dump value tables for 5-carat diamonds, find the same clarity and color grades as your stone, and note the price.

4. Divide that price by five. This will give you the per-carat price.

5. Multiply the per-carat price by the carat weight of the diamond you're looking at.

6. Increase that amount by the percentage listed in the following "Big Diamond Price Tables," and you'll have the general dump value of the stone.

7. Adjust for the class of the cut, and you'll have the true dump value.

For example, let's say we have a 7 ct, VS-1, G, Class 2-cut diamond:

- We look up a 5 ct, VS-1, G and find the price is $54,600.

- Divide $54,600 by 5, and we get a per-carat price of $10,920.

- Multiply 10,920 by 7 carats and we get $76,400.

- In the 7-carat Table, we find VS-1, G and see that we need to increase our price by 8.1%.

$$\$76,400 \times 0.081 = \mathbf{\$6,188.40}$$

$$\$76,400 + \$6,188.40 = \mathbf{\$82,588.40}$$

This is the general dump value of the diamond.

• We look up the cost adjustment for a Class 2-cut diamond and find that there is a 33% increase. The true dump value of our 7 ct, VS-1, G, Class 2 is $109,802.67.

The following tables show the approximate percentage of cost increase for diamonds larger than 5 carats:

BIG DIAMOND PRICE TABLES

6 CARAT STONES

COLOR	IF	VVS	VS	SI	I-1	I-2–I-3
D	2.6%	2.5%	2.4%	2.3%	2.2%	2.1%
E	2.4%	2.3%	2.2%	2.3%	2.2%	2.1%
F	2.4%	2.3%	2.2%	2.1%	2.1%	2.0%
G	2.2%	2.1%	2.1%	2.1%	2.1%	2.0%
H	2.2%	2.1%	2.1%	2.0%	2.0%	2.0%
I	2.0%	2.0%	2.0%	2.0%	2.0%	1.7%
J	2.0%	2.0%	2.0%	2.0%	2.0%	1.5%
K	2.0%	2.0%	2.0%	2.0%	2.0%	1.5%
L-M	1.4%	1.3%	1.2%	1.1%	1.0%	1.0%

7 CARAT STONES

COLOR	IF	VVS	VS	SI	I-1	I-2–I-3
D	7.7%	8.6%	8.3%	8.2%	6.6%	5.9%
E	7.6%	8.6%	8.3%	8.2%	6.5%	5.8%
F	7.6%	8.5%	8.2%	8.2%	6.5%	5.7%
G	7.5%	8.5%	8.1%	8.1%	6.4%	5.6%
H	7.5%	8.5%	8.1%	8.1%	6.3%	5.6%
I	7.0%	8.4%	8.0%	8.1%	6.2%	5.5%
J	7.0%	8.3%	8.0%	8.0%	6.0%	5.5%
K	6.5%	8.2%	8.0%	8.0%	6.0%	5.5%
L-M	5.5%	5.4%	5.3%	5.2%	5.1%	5.0%

BIG DIAMOND PRICE TABLES *(CONTINUED)*

8 CARAT STONES

COLOR	IF	VVS	VS	SI	I-1	I-2–I-3
D	8.8%	10.8%	10.7%	10.3%	7.8%	6.7%
E	8.8%	10.7%	10.7%	10.3%	7.7%	6.6%
F	8.8%	10.7%	10.5%	10.3%	7.7%	6.6%
G	8.7%	10.5%	10.5%	10.1%	7.6%	6.6%
H	8.7%	10.5%	10.5%	10.1%	7.6%	6.5%
I	8.5%	10.5%	10.4%	10.0%	7.5%	6.5%
J	8.5%	10.4%	10.4%	10.0%	7.5%	6.5%
K	8.1%	10.4%	10.3%	10.0%	7.5%	6.5%
L-M	6.6%	6.5%	6.4%	6.3%	6.2%	6.1%

9 CARAT STONES

COLOR	IF	VVS	VS	SI	I-1	I-2–I-3
D	15.5%	18.5%	18.5%	16.4%	13.0%	11.4%
E	15.5%	18.5%	18.4%	16.3%	13.0%	11.4%
F	15.5%	18.4%	18.3%	16.3%	13.0%	11.4%
G	15.4%	18.3%	18.3%	16.2%	12.9%	11.3%
H	15.4%	18.3%	18.3%	16.2%	12.8%	11.3%
I	14.6%	18.3%	18.2%	16.2%	12.8%	11.2%
J	14.5%	18.2%	18.2%	16.1%	12.7%	11.2%
K	14.2%	18.2%	18.0%	16.0%	12.7%	11.2%
L-M	11.5%	11.4%	11.3%	11.2%	11.1%	11.1%

BIG DIAMOND PRICE TABLES *(CONTINUED)*

10 CARAT STONES

COLOR	IF	VVS	VS	SI	I-1	I-2–I-3
D	26.2%	26.2%	26.2%	26.2%	24.8%	22.5%
E	26.2%	26.1%	26.1%	26.1%	24.8%	22.5%
F	26.1%	26.1%	27.5%	27.5%	24.8%	22.4%
G	26.1%	26.1%	27.2%	27.2%	24.6%	22.3%
H	26.1%	26.0%	27.1%	27.1%	24.6%	22.2%
I	26.0%	24.5%	25.0%	25.0%	24.5%	22.1%
J	26.0%	24.5%	25.0%	25.0%	24.5%	22.0%
K	26.0%	24.5%	24.8%	24.8%	24.2%	22.0%
L-M	21.6%	21.6%	21.5%	21.5%	21.3%	21.1%

Gem Trade Laboratories

Throughout the book I've referred to GIA, the Gemological Institute of America, as *the* diamond certification authority. This is because GIA was the first U.S. organization to provide lab certificates for diamonds. There are actually three certification centers in the United States regulated by the Federal Trade Commission:

> Gemological Institute of America
> 5345 Armada Drive
> Carlsbad, CA 92008
> (760) 603-4000

> Or

> Gemological Institute of America
> 580 5th Avenue, Suite 200
> New York, NY 10036-4794
> (212) 221-5858

156

European Gemological Laboratory, Inc.
550 South Hill Street, Suite 1565
Los Angeles, CA 90013-2414
(213) 622-2387

International Gemological Institute
579 5th Avenue, 7th Floor
New York, NY 10017
(212) 398-1700

*Diamond Guy Diamond Laboratory
4265 San Felipe Suite 960
Houston, TX 77027
(713) 222-2728

The Importance of Certification—Let's say, just for exam-ple, that you've purchased a diamond which *you* think is a par-ticular clarity grade and color grade, but the wizard you're trying to sell it to doesn't agree with you. Who's right? If you agree with *his* assessment, you won't make any money on the diamond and may even wind up losing money. What to do? This is where lab certification is very helpful. There isn't a wizard in the world who's going to argue with any one of the four FTC-regulated labs. A diamond with a certificate is like a pup with pedigree papers. Sometimes a certificate is the only way to settle a dispute and prove conclusively what you have. Fred's advice: *For any diamond with a wholesale value over $5,000, it's worth the $75–$500 invest-ment to get a certificate.* Certification prevents arguments with wizards and makes "Doing the Donald" quicker and easier.

Are All Labs Created Equal?—Yes and no. All four are reg-ulated by the FTC and are pretty much equal. But I have been

---

*I'm proud to say that I founded the D.G.D. Lab. I am also proud to say it is the strictest and hardest grading lab in existence. All diamonds are graded on the D.G.D. grading system that I invented and that allows very little leeway for error.

asked, if I had to choose *one* to certify a diamond, which one would it be? Well, that depends on what I plan to do with the diamond. Each of the labs has its pros and cons:

GIA	**Pros**

This was the first FTC-approved lab, and it still has the best international reputation. I think they have some of the toughest graders. If they say a diamond is D color, it is a *hard* D, which means there is no doubt or question. A soft grade means that a borderline diamond is bumped up to the higher grade. If I'm spending a lot of money on a VVS or flawless diamond, I want to know for sure if that stone is a D, E, or F. With a diamond as good as that, each color grade affects the value dramatically. If I'm buying a VS or SI in the F-G-H-I color range, it doesn't matter to me if the grade is hard or soft because one grade shift doesn't affect the price that much.

Cons
Even though GIA invented the classes of cut, they will not put the class of cut on a certificate. Nor will they give you the angles of the crown or the pavilion. Officially, they told me the reason is that their computers aren't programmed to print out that information. I think the reason is more political. GIA knows that most diamonds are not proportioned well, and if they printed that on their certificates, they might lose clients.

If you acquire a diamond with a GIA certificate, make sure your appraisal lists the crown angle and the pavilion angle, so all your bases are covered.

Summary   GIA is great for accurate clarity and color grades for investment-grade diamonds. GIA's turnaround time is 10 to 21 days. Average cost: $177.00.

EGL   **Pros**
EGL has a fine reputation, and they always give hard grades on SI-1's and VS-1's. When asked, they will break down the total depth percentage to give you the crown and pavilion angles, and will also tell you what class of cut a diamond is. I love these guys!

Cons
What's with this SI-3 grade? It is only a bumped-up I-1. Also, most of their split-graded diamonds (full-graded stones are the "1" grades in clarity; split-graded stones are the "2" grades), VVS-2, VS-2, and SI-2, and their I, J, and K color grades, are soft grades.

Summary   EGL is a terrific lab and is great about giving you proportion information when you ask. If they'd clean up their soft grades and dump the SI-3 grade, they'd be "King of the Hill." EGL's turn-around time is 3 to 5 days. Average cost: $100.00.

IGI **Pros**
Like EGL, this lab will break down the total depth and give you crown and pavilion angles when you ask. They will also tell you the class of cut. Their full-graded stones, VVS-1, VS-1, SI-1, and I-1, are always hard grades.

Cons
Their split-graded diamonds, VVS-2, VS-2, and SI-2, tend to be soft grades. Their color grades D through J also tend to be soft.

Summary First-rate. Great on checking proportions and full-graded stones. If they weren't so relaxed on the split grades, they'd be perfect. Turnaround time is 3 to 5 days. Average cost: $95.00.

DGD **Pros**
DGD is the newest of all the labs and doesn't have a long enough track record to become fairly graded against the other labs. However, sometimes the new kid in town is better than the old dog with a good track record. That is the case here. The DGD system has higher standards for grading clarity, color, and proportions than all the other labs combined. For example, some of the old labs still only use master sets to grade color, where DGD uses a high-tech colorimeter. For accuracy and the highest standards, a DGD certificate is unequaled!

Cons
There is no track record! They are brand spanking new! What if, as with a lot of new businesses, they go under a year or two from now? What will your DGD certificate be worth? I don't have a crystal ball, but I do know that time answers all questions.

Conclusion   For longevity and very good graders, as well as a reputation beyond reproach, it is hard not to pick the old dog GIA. But, if longevity is taken out of the equation, and accuracy, higher standards, and precision are your measuring stick, DGD leaves everyone in the dust!

Review

The most important things we covered in this chapter were (1) how to determine the true dump value of a diamond and (2) how proportion affects value. I hope you've learned a lot about doing the Sherlock Holmes, and you probably have. But don't think for a split second that you know all there is to know about judging the value of a diamond. As I said earlier, I recommend you take the GIA course in gemology and become certified in diamonds. There are also many books on the subject, and the GIA library in California has some that are well worth reading. Give them a call, and they'll send you a catalog free of charge. And if you're interested in learning more about acquiring diamonds on the primary market, not just the secondary or dump market, there's a brilliant book called *How to Buy a Diamond* by a guy named Fred Cuellar. I'm told it's the best in its field!

What's next? Believe it or not, our adventure is nearly over. In Chapter 9, we're off to meet the ultimate wizards, and in Chapter 10, a "bonus" chapter, we will learn the true meaning of "time is money!"

Dropsy
A Tale of Woe

The guy looked like a good customer—well dressed, neatly groomed. Could have been a hotshot commodities trader, young real-estate developer, something like that. Looked like he had some money and knew how to make a decision. Mid-to-late twenties, I guessed. He wanted to look at some one-carat loose diamonds.

As I was showing him a tray of stones, going through my usual patter about the four C's, he held up his hand to interrupt me. Then he singled out one stone, placed his finger on it, and said, "That one. I'll take it."

Well, well, I thought. Decision maker, indeed. And a good judge of quality. The diamond he had chosen was a very good one, VS-1, E color.

"I'll give you a thousand dollars cash to hold it for me," he said. "I'll bring my girlfriend in tomorrow to look at it and give her approval. I don't see any problem with that," he said with a quick smile.

I didn't see any problem with that, either. Next day he showed up with girl, as promised. She was a knockout, too, worth every point, grade, and facet of that diamond, I thought. She held the diamond, saw it sparkle, felt the weight of its full one carat, and pronounced it perfect. As she was handing it back to me, our hands bumped and the diamond dropped to the carpet.

The young man quickly bent to retrieve it, apologizing as he returned it to my hand, and could we pick up the finished ring in two weeks?

"No problem," I said, folding the stone into a paper parcel for next-day delivery to my "benchman," the guy who makes my jewelry and sets the stones.

Two days later the benchman called.

"Fred," he said, "this one-carat you sent for mounting? It's a C-Z. You knew that, right?"

A C-Z? A worthless cubic zirconia? What had happened to the VS-1, E diamond?

It came to me in a flashback, a slow-motion replay. I watched my diamond fall from the beautiful girl's hand, down to the carpet, landing softly, out of my line of sight. Then the young man, bending down quickly, a practiced move, palming my diamond, handing me the cubic zirconia, smiling, apologizing. I'd been conned by a simple switcheroo.

They were good, I'll grant you that. Their thousand-dollar cash deposit gave me the sense of security they knew it would, and after that I was a toy in their game.

Never again. And you, my friend, if ever a diamond leaves your sight, immediately weigh it and check it to make sure you haven't been scammed.

A wise man once said,
"Experience is a good school, but the fees are high."

"DOING THE DONALD"— ADVANCED LEVEL

Okay, you've come this far with me, so let me ask you a question: What's the most difficult part of this enterprise? Is it the Treasure Hunt, the Sherlock Holmes, or "Doing the Donald?"

If you answered "Treasure Hunt," you're absolutely right. If you follow my guidelines and work hard, your treasure chest will fill up, all right, but the Treasure Hunt is without a doubt the toughest part of the game. Why? There are so many crummy diamonds out there, that's why! And as this book becomes popular, and more and more people find out about the true liquidation value of jewelry and learn how to find it and sell it, great deals will get harder to find. But don't panic—this book will have to sell a few million copies for that to happen, and that could take years. And not everyone who buys and reads this book will be as diligent and hardworking as you are, so don't be afraid of a little competition.

Pay close attention now. I'm going to tell you one of the most important lessons in this chapter and, in fact, in the whole book: *The number one rookie mistake is selling your treasure too quickly!*

If you're going to get rich in the diamond business, selling at dump will always be your last resort. Not your first—your *last*. Always.

Keep in mind that there are a *lot* of people out there willing to pay *retail* for diamonds. *Retail!* That's twice wholesale. Many of those people would love to buy your treasure just to get *any* break off retail. So would the brotherly wizards we discussed earlier, your family and friends. People who are deal seekers could not care *less* that you're selling previously owned jewelry. What they *do* care about is seeing their dollars go further.

We will call these bargain hounds our *ultimate wizards.*

Selling to the general public is fantastic business. John Q. Public is our very first choice when we're seeking a buyer for our treasure. You see, we can offer him treasure at *66% above dump value*—which is wholesale—and he'll think it's better than sex! (Well. . . .)

The trick is to let the public know who you are, what you have to offer, and how to find you. That's what we're going to learn—how to reach out to ultimate wizards so they can buy your treasure. Once we've learned that *all new treasure gets shopped first to ultimate wizards,* and second to brotherly wizards, then only when all else fails do we sell at dump value. Following this three-step process will guarantee we'll get the most for our treasure and thus make the most money we possibly can.

Reaching the Ultimate Wizards

Three words: *Print, radio, and television.* I have found that these three media are very effective ways to reach ultimate wizards.

Print—The best thing about print advertising is, it's *cheap!* I like to start with print, and when the money comes rolling in, I move up to radio and TV.

The first ad we're going to place will be in our *local newspaper.* It will look very similar to the ad we created for the Treasure Hunt, but this one will be targeted to ultimate wizards. When people go shopping for jewelry, they have two main concerns:

1. Getting good merchandise.

2. Getting the best possible price.

Our ad has to speak to these concerns. We need to let the buyers know that we have the top-quality merchandise they're looking for and we're offering it at an unbelievable price.

Take a look at these two ads. Which one do you think will motivate our ultimate wizard to pick up the phone and call us?

Talk about a no-brainer—the first ad, right? *Just Kidding!* Obviously the second ad is the one that will make the phone ring. But why? Let's analyze the first ad for a moment. For starters, the first line: "Diamonds for Sale." What kind of diamonds? What quality? What price? This first line leaves us with more questions than answers. The next line: "Various sizes and shapes." What does that tell us? What sizes? What shapes? Again, lots of unanswered questions. And who's this "Bud" dude? What kind of credibility or certification would a guy named "Bud" have? Sounds like a shady operator to me. Will I call him? As the kids say, "As if!"

Now let's consider the second ad, a thing of beauty and a joy forever: "ACTUAL LAB CERTIFIED GIA APPRAISED DIAMONDS." This tells my reader that these stones come with a pedigree, even if he doesn't know what GIA is. It says the quality of my diamonds is guaranteed: "All Shapes, Sizes, and Quality SOLD BELOW WHOLESALE!!!" That says, "You want it? I've got it!" One-stop shopping.

"But, Fred," you're saying, "I *don't* have everything! Aren't I telling my customer a fib?" No! A little later on I'm going to teach you about setting up "wizard accounts" and getting diamonds on the primary market to fill in gaps in your inventory to satisfy customers. So while you may not have "everything" in your hot little hand, you *do* have virtually everything within your reach. If you need it, you can get it. If a potential buyer reads that ad and sees that you have "everything," he'll be more confident in you, *and* he knows you'll make life easier for him. And isn't that what folks want? People are inherently lazy! They want instant gratification—instant breakfast, fast food, short lines.

That line also promises "BELOW WHOLESALE" prices. Everyone wants something for nothing, right? You do, I do, we all do. But we don't mind doing a little work for our share. By saying "BELOW WHOLESALE" you're not committing to an exact price but you *are* implying, "Hey, pal, you just can't get a better deal than this!"

"Satisfaction Guaranteed!" I love this line! You're telling the reader that the customer is always right, and unless he's happy he doesn't pay a dime. That's a lot of mileage from two words. And remember, you have nothing to lose by guaranteeing satisfaction because you actually are giving someone a good deal. If you give a customer his money back, you still have the diamond, and you can sell it to someone else.

Finally, "DIAMOND BROKERS U.S.A." Of course, you don't use *those* words, you insert your own company's name and number. Just remember, when you name your company, the name should command integrity, respect, and trust.

Our next print medium is the good old *Yellow Pages*. Over the past decade, no single form of print advertising has been more successful for me that the Yellow Pages. In fact, I would recommend that you time the opening of your new business to coincide with the new Yellow Pages directory hitting the streets with your ad inside.

There's some basic information a reader must get from a successful Yellow Pages ad:

1. Your company name.

2. Location.

3. Hours of operation (Example: Mon–Fri, 9–6, Sat 9–5).

4. "By appointment only"—I know this sounds kind of snooty, and you may be wondering why I want you to discourage walk-ins, but think about this for a moment. *First*, by requiring an appointment, you get a more serious buyer. *Second*, when you're just starting out in business, you're not going to have a lot of employees. What would you do if seven customers walked in at about the same time? Six would end up waiting, and some of them would get mad and walk out, and you'd never see them again. *Third*, by setting up appointments, you can leave enough time between clients that you'll never rush anyone. And *fourth*, you're a professional! Would you think of seeing your doctor or attorney without an appointment? Not unless it

were an emergency. They're professionals, and so are you. Act like one.

5. Forms of payment you accept (Mastercard, Visa, Amex, and so forth).

6. Type of inventory (Example: "All sizes and shapes, ¼ ct to 5 ct").

7. A reference about quality and price, the same as in your newspaper ad.

8. Telephone number—in **bold type.**

You should place this ad in *three places* in the Yellow Pages: "Diamonds, Wholesale"; "Jewelers, Retail"; and "Appraisers."

Okay, Fred, the first two make absolute sense, but "Appraisers"? Yes, and let me tell you why. There are a lot of people who get jewelry appraised when they're planning to sell it, and there are people who get merchandise appraised when they're thinking of buying it. At $25 to $50 a pop, it brings in some pocket money, you may wind up with the merchandise they're planning to sell, or you might make a new friend/client by advising a would-be buyer that he's being overcharged for something. (*Note:* It is unlawful to advertise yourself as an appraiser unless you are GIA-certified.)

Sample Ad for "Diamonds, Wholesale" Section and "Jewelers, Retail" Section

DIAMOND BROKERS USA
All Diamonds Lab Certified & GIA Appraised

- SOLD BELOW WHOLESALE!
- *All Shapes & Sizes ¼ ct to 5 ct*
- SATISFACTION GUARANTEED!

By Appointment Only
Mon–Fri 9:00 to 9:00   777 Yellow Brick Road
Sat & Sun 12:00 to 5:00   NY, NY 10000
Telephone: (555) 555-5555

Sample Ad for "Appraisers" Section

DIAMOND BROKERS USA
Jewelry Appraisal Services

- Appraisal While You Wait
- Full Gem Lab
- Satisfaction Guaranteed

By Appointment Only
Mon–Fri 9:00 to 9:00   777 Yellow Brick Road
Sat & Sun 12:00 to 5:00   NY, NY 10000
Telephone: (555) 555-5555

172

People are always in a hurry, so let them know you can do the job while they wait. (If they've read this book, they wouldn't leave their diamonds with you, anyway!)

The "Full Gem Lab" reference assures them that you have the equipment to do the job right.

The last type of print ads we'll deal with are *national magazines and newspapers.* This is going to be a very short lesson: *Stay away!*

Concentrate on local advertising. Sure, a lot of people read *USA Today* and *People Magazine,* but how many of them are going to travel out of their home area to buy a diamond from you? I'll give you a hint: It's a round number. There might come a day when you want to begin regional or national advertising, especially if you open offices in other cities. But at this stage of your new career, national advertising is a bottomless money pit. Don't throw *your* hard-won dollars into it—you'll never see them again.

Radio—This is a great medium. *Everyone* listens to the radio, and it can be a wonderful way to let ultimate wizards know about you. But there are right and wrong ways to use radio. The right way is to use a *media planner* (or *media buyer*), and the wrong way is to do it yourself.

I did it myself. Oh, yeah, old Fred was too smart to hire an agency to do what he thought he could do himself. I wrote the ads, I chose the radio stations, I bought the time slots, I monitored the results—and I made the radio stations $100,000 richer over six months and got a very expensive lesson in advertising. What was I doing wrong? I'd hear all these radio ads for other local companies and couldn't understand how they could afford it. It took me eleven years to figure it out, and the answer was right under my nose: *Media planners.* While I had been paying the absolute highest rate at every radio station because I was a *little guy,* the other local advertisers I was hearing were, in effect, *getting it wholesale* by using media planners. Media planners are found in advertising agencies. They get cheaper rates because they buy in bulk, using the combined buying power of hundreds of little guys like me, so the radio stations don't treat them like little guys.

Not only do radio stations give you cheaper rates when you work through an agency's media planner, they give you *value-added service*—that means freebies, bonus spots at no cost, a morning show host endorsing your product—all the ingredients you need to make radio work for you and to bring the ultimate wizards to your doorstep. Furthermore, radio stations build into their rates *free production services.* That means they'll write and produce your spots for free, using their in-house talent.

Two other things I learned about radio: *Location* and *frequency.* By "location" I not only mean which radio station, but which *day part,* or time of day. "Frequency" refers not to the station's position on the dial, but how often your ads run.

First, your message has to be placed on the stations that are going to reach *your customer.* You can probably draw a fairly good profile of your customer for the media planner, or he or she can probably draw it for you on the basis of past experience. Every radio station has its own format, and each format reaches a slightly different audience in terms of age, gender, income, and so forth. The media planners will know where your ads should go.

Second, the time of day is important. Advertising rates are highest in radio's prime time, morning drive, because that's when the station reaches the most people. With the media planner, figure out what you can afford in terms of the *day part* you advertise in. (Don't buy the *cheapo* time slot from midnight to 5 A.M. just because it is so cheap. It's cheap because no one's listening.)

Decide how often you want your spots to run and for how many weeks. Radio stations operate on 13-week cycles, and it will take more than one cycle to make a lasting impression on the listeners. Here's a schedule that has worked for me:

Weeks 1 and 2:	Buy morning drive (6–9 A.M.) on the top three stations that reach the 18–34 market. Run your ad three times a week.
Week 3:	Take a break.
Weeks 4 through 13:	Same schedule as above, *every other week.*

Depending on your market size, this schedule might cost you $8,000 to $10,000 a month. Gasp! Hang in there—it will pay off! In the first quarter (three months), you'll be lucky to break even. In the second quarter, you *should* break even. In the third quarter, you should make a 50% return on your investment, and from that point on you should be getting a 2-for-1 return, meaning that for every dollar you spend on radio advertising you'll take in two.

But be smart about it! I've already paid for this lesson, and there's no point in you paying all over again. Use a media planner and pay attention to where your $$$ goes. Remember, *a dollar not spent is a dollar earned!*

Television—This is the most powerful advertising medium in the world, and also the most expensive. Forget national TV—way too expensive. But advertising on your local stations and on cable can be affordable and profitable. Again, work with your friendly media planner, who will negotiate the deals with the TV stations and the local cable supplier. If you're comfortable in front of the camera, star in your own commercials. People feel better about dealing with someone they've seen on TV. Don't let your ego make this decision—ask the media planner for honest advice.

A Television Primer

A quick sketch of the television landscape. Not too long ago, before our communities were all cabled, we received TV through the air. We had our rooftop antenna, or at least rabbit ears, and we would tune in the three or four local stations. When cable came along, a whole new world opened up. How it works is that your local cable system imports programming, usually by satellite, from a variety of sources. Your local cable supplier not only carries your local over-the-air stations, but also a lot of other channels that are *not* broadcast over the air, but are available only on cable—such as A&E, or ESPN, and CNN. Your local cable supplier brings all this programming in to their site, called a *head end*, and distributes it through a wire to your home and the homes of other subscribers in the community. The community is granted one or two channels by the cable supplier for *local access* programming, and this is usually community-oriented programming and free of advertising.

You can buy advertising time on both the over-the-air stations in your market and on the cable system. You can buy time on a national cable service like CNN and have your ad seen only on your local cable system. Talk with your media planner.

Review

Structure your plan of attack along the lines I've presented here. Conquer the print first and become profitable before moving into radio. Give radio at least a year before moving into TV. If you plan well and have patience, all the treasure you buy will end up being sold to ultimate wizards—the *general public*—and you'll visit the dump wizards as little as possible.

Wizard Review and Wizard Accounts

1. *What's a "wizard"?*—Anyone who buys our treasure.

2. *What are the types of wizards?*—*Regular, brotherly,* and *ultimate.*

3. *What's a "regular wizard"?*—Anyone who buys our treasure at dump value. Also called a *"dump wizard."*

4. *Who are the most common dump wizards?*—Jewelers, pawn-shops, diamond dealers clubs, and the New York Diamond Dealers Club.

5. *What's a "brotherly wizard"?*—A family member or close friend who buys our treasure, usually at 20% above dump value.

6. *What's an "ultimate wizard"?*—A member of the general public, who buys our treasure at wholesale, which is dump value plus 66%.

7. *Which is the first wizard we try to sell our treasure to?*—An ultimate wizard.

8. *How long should we try to sell a treasure to an ultimate wizard or a brotherly wizard before visiting a dump wizard?*—Two months.

9. *What's the number one mistake?*—Selling treasure too quickly to a brotherly wizard or a dump wizard before we have an opportunity to sell to an ultimate wizard for a much higher profit.

10. *What do we do when an ultimate wizard asks for a piece of treasure that's not in our inventory?*—We get the item from our "wizard account." A *wizard account* is simply an arrangement you make with one or two diamond dealers in your area, who can supply merchandise when you get a request for a diamond you don't have. When you establish relationships with dump wizards, try to work out an arrangement in which they'll sell you diamonds when you need them, ideally at 10% below wholesale. Don't expect them

to sell to you at dump prices. Then, a fair price to charge an ultimate wizard for an item from a wizard account would be 10% above wholesale.

Conclusion

That's it, my friend. I've taught you everything that I set out to teach you; now the rest is up to you. If at any time you get confused about something, *call my Help Line!* I mean it! That's why the Help Line is there.

Use this book as a road map to riches. Just as with any road map, though, this book can only show you the way—it's not a magic carpet that will take you there. You have to supply the means, the motivation, the will power, and the horsepower to take yourself as far as you want to go.

I wish you great success, and a lot of fun along the way. You've already given me a reward by buying this book, but my greatest reward will be knowing that I've helped you achieve your dreams.

Sincerely,

Fred Cuellar

Getting Started Checklist

Getting Started

A Check-List for Major Leaguers

__ Read book

__ Read book again

__ Get GIA-certified (Chapter 7)

__ Lay the foundation (Chapter 7)

__ Reach out to Brotherly Wizards (Chapter 6)

__ Line up "Deal of a Lifetime" backers (Chapter 7)

__ Begin Treasure Hunting (Chapters 1, 4, and 7)

__ Reach out to Ultimate Wizards (Chapter 9)

__ Advertise in the Yellow Pages (Chapter 9)

__ Create Wizard Accounts (Chapter 9)

What Am I Bid?
A Story of Sweet Success

You know the old joke: Sometimes you have to kiss a lot of frogs before one turns into a prince. Estate auctions are like that. They may *look* like frogs, but one may turn out to be a prince in disguise.

At the preview of one of the many estate auctions I've attended, I noticed an odd-looking ring. The stone appeared a dingy yellow, and it was set in white metal. White gold? Platinum, perhaps? I asked the auctioneer what he knew about the ring.

"It's a 'golden beryl,'" he told me, "and I've set an opening bid of $50." But as I looked at the ring I felt a tingle, a suspicion. I asked for a closer look.

Holding my breath, I examined the ring under my loupe. Inside the setting I saw the word "Plat." stamped in tiny letters. My heartbeat quickened. I examined the stone. The first thing I saw was an inclusion that was definitely not typical of a beryl, "golden" or otherwise. It was a diamond, and a big one! I tried to appear bored and uninterested as I handed the ring back to the auctioneer, but now my pulse was really pounding. I took my seat and waited for the item to come up for bid, hoping no one else had seen what I had seen!

Finally the auctioneer held up the ring in its box.

"Item Number 134, a pretty little golden beryl ring. Let's start the bidding on this little beauty at $50. Do I hear $50?"

I made no move to bid, not wanting to arouse the suspicions of any of the other bidders. No one raised a bidding paddle.

"C'mon, folks. Clean her up a little and this could be a beautiful ring. Who'll bid $40 for the golden beryl ring?"

With what I hoped was a casual shrug and a smile, I raised my numbered paddle.

"I have a bid of $40. Thank you, sir. Do I hear $50? No? Going once at $40, twice at $40 . . . *sold* to the man for $40."

When I got my treasure home and cleaned it, the gem really began to sparkle. I performed a full appraisal—weight, clarity, color, cut, the whole process—then sat back and admired my new treasure. It was a rare canary diamond, 4.86 carats, in a platinum setting. Value? $33,800!

Brothers and sisters, keep kissin' those frogs.

CHAPTER TEN

BONUS!

"TIME" TO MAKE MORE MONEY

Folks, I could probably fill another book telling you every-thing you need to know about making money with watches. And there is money to be made, believe me. In a nut-shell, you follow the same basic principles that I've taught you about making money with diamonds: (1) know your watches, so you'll know what you're dealing with; (2) know the dump values of the watches; (3) buy at below dump; and (4) sell at above dump.

On the following pages you'll find dump tables for what I believe to be the best and most valuable watches in the world. The tables list the current retail prices, current wholesale prices, and *three* dump values, based on the condition of the watch.

A warning: Selling your watch for cash can be very com-plicated. The wizards you sell diamonds to are of little use because the demand for high-end watches comes nowhere near the demand for diamonds. There are perhaps a half-dozen places in the United States that will pay top dollar for your watch. For my money, the very best of these is Tarrytown Jewelers, founded in 1972 by world-renowned, classic watch expert Steven Dubinsky and his wife Marlene. I believe they are the top vendors and distributors of fine watches in the world. If you ever need help in disposing of or acquiring a fine watch, there's no one better to call on:

Tarrytown Jewelers
273 N. Central Avenue
Hartsdale, NY 10530
(800) 522-2161 or
(914) 949-0481

Many firms today produce fine and complex wrist watches. In addition to telling time, phases of the moon, chronographs, and repeaters, some signal the time with ear-pleasing chimes, activated at your command. All of these features add value and cost to a watch, and result in a highly complex assemblage of gears, wheels, springs, and jewels designed to take the fine art of horology to its highest levels.

While there are many firms producing complicated watches, most simply incorporate the designs and mechanics of the past. Only a few firms, some of them founded in the 18th century, operate on the leading edges of watchmaking design and technology. Throughout many decades of setting the highest standards, producing timepieces for royalty and the most discriminating clientele, these firms have remained at the head of an ever-growing class of watchmakers. The watches produced by these leading firms are the most sought after by collectors, and consequently fetch the highest prices when they change hands—or, perhaps more accurately, change wrists.

Fine *pocket watches* continue to enjoy popularity among collectors, but wrist-watch prices have soared during the past twenty years, firmly establishing themselves as good investments and marketable commodities.

Steven Dubinsky has described and evaluated the leading watch brands for us. Each watchmaker's address and telephone number is listed at the top of its dump value tables, and I'm sure all of them would be happy to send you brochures and catalogs of their watches so that you'll be able to match a picture with a dump table or identify each model when you see it.

Steve has also compiled for us a list of the Top 20 most collectible watches in the world. If you're curious as to whether Granddad's old pocket watch is worth a small fortune, take a close look at that list.

The World's Finest Watchmakers

Audemars Piguet
The house of Audemars Piguet, founded in the 19th century, produces some of the world's finest timepieces, including repeaters, chronographs, and perpetual calendars. Better known abroad than in the United States, an Audemars Piguet ranks among the best and most sought-after watches in the world.

Bertolucci
While enjoying modest popularity as a fashionable timepiece, Bertolucci's watches tend to depreciate rather quickly. I don't recommend them as an investment or for good trade-in value.

Breguet

These are perhaps the most elegant of all the fine watches being made today. The distinctive enameled silver dial of each Breguet watch is etched with its own serial number, as has been done since the firm's inception in the nineteenth century. Although the company makes several types of complicated watches, each is unmistakably a Breguet by virtue of its distinctive appearance. Commissioned by royalty and the discriminating, Breguet is one of the finest watchmakers in the world.

Breitling

The company's moderately priced wrist watches are excellent values, considering their durable cases and movements, and solid sense of style. Extremely popular with navigators, Breitling is best known for its fine chronographs, many of which are self-winding and available in steel, gold, and combined metals.

Cartier

Admired more for its sense of style than for its horological attributes, Cartier has defined wrist-watch styling in the twentieth century. As with its fine jewelry, anything bearing the Cartier name should hold its value well. Although its watches are primarily produced in quartz today, Cartier remains a favorite of collectors.

Corum

Although this company produces mostly quartz watches, Corum has established its own line of classics with its various coin and ingot watches, which enjoy a good deal of popularity.

Ebel

With strong sales in the United States. and abroad, Ebel has established itself as a leading watchmaker. However, only a few of its models, such as the Belugas and some sports models, perform well in the trade arena.

Patek Philippe

What Rolls Royce is to fine motor cars, Patek Philippe is to fine watches: Simply the best. In more than 150 years of watchmaking, the firm has established an untarnished reputation for the highest quality movements combined with elegant, superlative design. Patek Philippe timepieces continue to set auction-house records with sales of repeaters, world-time pieces, chronographs, and perpetual calendars.

Rolex

Probably the most popular of today's high-end watches in terms of sheer sales numbers, Rolex stands out for its classic style, waterproof oyster case, lock-down crown, and durable self-winding movement. A modern-day status symbol, both contemporary and period Rolexes dating back to the 1920s adorn many collectors' wrists.

Vacheron Constantin

This old Swiss house produces some of the finest and most sought-after wrist watches in the world. From the simple elegance of one of its time-only watches, to the sophistication of its perpetual calendars and other complicated pieces, Vacheron stands out as a world leader in horology.

WATCH DUMP VALUE TABLES

Cartier Inc.
Two Corporate Drive #440
Shelton, CT 06484-6234
(202) 925-6400

SANTOS

	RETAIL	WHOLESALE	DUMP PRICES EXCELLENT	GOOD	FAIR
MENS SANTOS STAINLESS STEEL	$2,200	$1,210	$770	$660	$550
LADIES SANTOS STAINLESS STEEL	$2,100	$1,155	$735	$630	$525
MENS SANTOS TWO-TONE	$3,200	$1,760	$1,120	$960	$800
LADIES SANTOS TWO-TONE	$3,100	$1,705	$1,085	$930	$775
SANTOS ROUND FACE STAINLESS STEEL AND 18K					
LARGE	$3,600	$1,980	$1,260	$1,080	$900
MEDIUM	$3,350	$1,842	$1,172	$1,005	$837
SANTOS ROUND FACE STAINLESS STEEL					
LARGE	$2,600	$1,430	$910	$780	$650
MEDIUM	$2,350	$1,292	$822	$705	$587
MENS SANTOS ROUND FACE 18K GOLD	$19,400	$10,670	$6,790	$5,820	$4,850
LADIES SANTOS ROUND FACE 18K GOLD	$19,400	$10,670	$6,790	$5,820	$4,850

188

PANTHERE

	RETAIL	WHOLESALE	DUMP PRICES		
			EXCELLENT	GOOD	FAIR
MENS PANTHERE STAINLESS STEEL	$2,400	$1,320	$840	$720	$600
LADIES PANTHERE STAINLESS STEEL	$2,200	$1,210	$770	$660	$550
MENS PANTHERE TWO-TONE	$5,200	$2,860	$1,820	$1,560	$1,300
LADIES PANTHERE TWO-TONE	$4,450	$2,447	$1,557	$1,335	$1,112
MENS PANTHERE 18K GOLD	$16,300	$8,965	$5,705	$4,890	$4,075
LADIES PANTHERE 18K GOLD	$11,400	$6,270	$3,990	$3,420	$2,850

TANK

	RETAIL	WHOLESALE	DUMP PRICES		
			EXCELLENT	GOOD	FAIR
MENS TANK FRANCAISE STAINLESS STEEL	$2,700	$1,485	$945	$810	$675
LADIES TANK FRANCAISE STAINLESS STEEL	$2,400	$1,320	$840	$720	$600
MENS TANK FRANCAISE TWO-TONE	$4,200	$2,310	$1,050	$1,260	$1,050
LADIES TANK FRANCAISE TWO-TONE	$3,700	$2,035	$1,295	$1,110	$925
MENS TANK FRANCAISE 18K GOLD	$18,520	$10,186	$6,482	$5,556	$4,630
LADIES TANK FRANCAISE 18K GOLD	$11,400	$6,290	$3,990	$3,420	$2,850

PASHA

	RETAIL	WHOLESALE	DUMP PRICES		
			EXCELLENT	GOOD	FAIR
PASHA 35MM STAINLESS STEEL	$3,150	$1,732	$1,102	$945	$787
PASHA 38MM TWO-TONE					
STRAP	$5,000	$2,750	$1,750	$1,500	$1,250
BRACELET	$6,000	$3,300	$2,100	$1,800	$1,500
PASHA 38MM STAINLESS STEEL	$4,750	$2,612	$1,662	$1,425	$1,187
PASHA 35MM 18K GOLD					
STRAP	$9,900	$5,445	$3,465	$2,970	$2,475
BRACELET	$19,900	$10,945	$6,965	$5,970	$4,975

Rolex Watch USA Inc.
665 Fifth Ave.
New York, NY 10022-5305
(212) 758-7700

	RETAIL	WHOLESALE	DUMP PRICES		
			EXCELLENT	GOOD	FAIR
MENS PRESIDENT DAY-DATE 18K	$15,900	$9,540	$7,155	$6,360	$5,565
LADIES PRESIDENT DAY-DATE 18K	$11,750	$7,050	$5,287	$4,700	$4,112
MENS TWO-TONE DATE JUST	$5,300	$3,180	$2,385	$2,120	$1,855
LADIES TWO-TONE DATE JUST	$4,200	$2,520	$1,890	$1,680	$1,470
SUBMARINER 18K GOLD DATE	$19,250	$11,550	$8,662	$7,700	$6,737
SUBMARINER TWO-TONE DATE	$5,800	$3,480	$2,610	$6,636	$2,030
SEA DWELLER 4000 DATE STAINLESS STEEL	$3,600	$2,160	$1,620	$1,440	$1,260
GMT MASTER I STAINLESS STEEL	$3,300	$1,980	$1,485	$1,320	$1,155
GMT MASTER II DATE STAINLESS STEEL	$3,500	$2,100	$1,575	$1,400	$1,225
MENS DATE JUST STAINLESS STEEL	$2,975	$1,785	$1,338	$1,190	$1,041
LADIES DATE JUST STAINLESS STEEL	$2,725	$1,635	$1,226	$1,090	$953
EXPLORER II DATE STAINLESS STEEL	$3,275	$1,965	$1,473	$1,310	$1,146
MENS 18K YACHTMASTER	$19,250	$11,550	$8,662	$7,700	$6,737
MENS 18K DAYTONA	$20,450	$12,270	$9,202	$8,180	$7,157
MENS STAINLESS STEEL DAYTONA	$5,100	$3,060	$5,000	$4,500	$4,000

Bertolucci
201 Rt. 17 North 18th Floor
Rutherford, NJ 07070
(201) 507-4400

	RETAIL	WHOLESALE	DUMP PRICES		
			EXCELLENT	GOOD	FAIR
VIR GENTS WATCH					
124 55 41 127 STAINLESS STEEL	$3,050	$1,677	$762	$610	$457
124 55 49 220 TWO-TONE	$5,250	$2,887	$1,312	$1,050	$787
124 55 68 221 18K STRAP	$6,300	$3,465	$1,575	$1,260	$945
VIR CHRONOGRAPH WATCH					
664 55 41 187 STAINLESS STEEL	$4,200	$2,310	$1,050	$840	$945
664 55 49 280 TWO-TONE	$6,300	$3,465	$1,575	$1,260	$945
664 50 68 282 18K STRAP	$8,000	$4,400	$2,000	$1,600	$1,200
MARIS DIVERS WATCH					
629 55 41 1D0 STAINLESS STEEL	$3,350	$1,842	$837	$670	$502
629 55 49 2D4 TWO-TONE	$4,200	$2,310	$1,050	$840	$630
629 55 49 2D3 TWO-TONE	$7,600	$4,180	$1,900	$1,520	$1,140
VIR LADIES WATCH					
094 55 41 127 STAINLESS STEEL	$2,950	$1,622	$737	$590	$502
094 55 49 227 TWO-TONE	$9,100	$5,005	$2,275	$1,820	$1,365
094 55 68 621 18K	$13,800	$7,590	$3,450	$2,760	$2,070
VIR MINI WATCH					
083 55 41 120 STAINLESS STEEL	$2,550	$1,237	$637	$570	$382
083 55 49 221 TWO-TONE	$3,600	$1,980	$900	$720	$540
083 33 68 671 18K	$13,500	$7,425	$3,375	$2,700	$2,025

Corum
North American Watch Corp.
125 Chub Ave.
Lynhurst, NJ 07071-3504
(201) 460-4800

	RETAIL	WHOLESALE	DUMP PRICES		
			EXCELLENT	GOOD	FAIR
50 145 56 0000 MU51 GENTS 20 US$ STRAP WATCH, QUARTZ	$7,990	$4,394	$2,397	$1,997	$1,598
50 148 56 V041 MU31 GENTS 10 US$ BRACELET WATCH, QUARTZ	$16,900	$9,295	$5,070	$4,225	$3,380
50 486 65 0000 MU17 GENTS 5 US$ STRAP WATCH, DIAMONDS, QUARTZ	$11,900	$6,545	$3,570	$2,975	$2,380
30 300 56 0000 MU16 LADIES 5 US$ STRAP WATCH, QUARTZ	$5,500	$3,025	$1,650	$1,375	$1,100
50 497 56 0000 MU33 GENTS 10 US$ STRAP WATCH, QUARTZ	$6,990	$3,844	$2,097	$1,747	$1,398
50 147 56 0000 MU31 GENTS 10 US$ STRAP WATCH, QUARTZ	$6,490	$3,569	$1,947	$1,622	$1,298
50 146 56 M138 MU51 GENTS 20 US$ BRACELET WATCH, QUARTZ	$19,000	$10,450	$5,700	$4,750	$3,800
30 301 56 M138 MU16 LADIES 5 US$ BRACELET WATCH, QUARTZ	$14,900	$8,195	$4,470	$3,725	$2,900

Ebel
750 Lexington Ave.
New York, NY 10022
(212) 888-3235

BELUGA

	RETAIL	WHOLESALE	DUMP PRICES		
			EXCELLENT	GOOD	FAIR
REF #: 884 960/3502, MENS QUARTZ, 18K GOLD, CROCODILE STRAP	$6,000	$3,300	$2,160	$1,800	$1,500
REF #: 866 960/5022, LADIES QUARTZ, 18K GOLD BRACELET, MOTHER OF PEARL DIAL	$10,650	$5,857	$3,727	$3,195	$2,662
REF #: 866 969-5029, LADIES QUARTZ, 18K GOLD BRACELET, DIAMOND STUDDED CASE, MOTHER OF PEARL DIAMOND DIAL	$16,500	$9,075	$5,775	$4,950	$4,125

SPORT CLASSIC

	RETAIL	WHOLESALE	DUMP PRICES		
			EXCELLENT	GOOD	FAIR
REF #: 1187 141/2502, MENS QUARTZ, STEEL AND GOLD WAVE BRACELET	$1,975	$1,086	$691	$592	$493
REF #: 1087 121/2592, LADIES QUARTZ, STEEL AND 18K GOLD WAVE BRACELET, MOTHER OF PEARL DIAL	$1,900	$1,045	$665	$570	$475
REF #: 1057 901/2502, MINI QUARTZ, STEEL AND 18K GOLD WAVE BRACELET	$1,500	$825	$525	$450	$375
REF #: 8057 901/60 02PP, MINI QUARTZ, 18K GOLD LINK BRACELET, WHITE ROMAN DIAL	$8,950	$4,922	$3,132	$2,685	$2,237
REF #: 8057 902/60 99PP, MINI QUARTZ, 18K GOLD LINK BRACELET, DIAMOND BEZEL, MOTHER OF PEARL DIAMOND DIAL	$12,450	$6,847	$4,357	$3,735	$3,112
REF #: 1057 901-60P, MINI QUARTZ, STEEL AND 18K GOLD LINK BRACELET, MOTHER OF PEARL DIAL	$2,400	$1,320	$840	$720	$600
REF #: 1057 902/25099, MINI QUARTZ, STEEL AND GOLD WAVE BRACELET, DIAMOND BEZEL, MOTHER OF PEARL DIAMOND DIAL	$5,000	$2,750	$1,750	$1,500	$1,250
REF #: 9087132/40 174P, MENS QUARTZ, HIGH+ POLISHED STEEL WAVE BRACELET	$1,550	$852	$542	$465	$387
REF #: 9187142/40 52P, MENS LARGE QUARTZ, HIGH POLISHED STEEL WAVE BRACELET	$1,550	$852	$542	$465	$387
REF #: 9157115/40 179P, MINI QUARTZ, DIAMOND BEZEL, HIGH+ POLISHED STEEL WAVE BRACELET	$3,250	$1,787	$1,137	$975	$812
REF #: 91571121/40 135P, MINI QUARTZ, HIGH POLISHED STEEL WAVE BRACELET	$1,450	$797	$507	$435	$362

1911

	RETAIL	WHOLESALE	DUMP PRICES		
			EXCELLENT	GOOD	FAIR
REF #: 1080916/60 02P, MENS LARGE, AUTOMATIC, STEEL AND 18K GOLD LINK BRACELET	$4,750	$2,612	$1,662	$1,425	$1,187
REF #: 887902/35 02D, MENS QUARTZ, 18K GOLD CROCODILE STRAP	$5,550	$3,052	$1,942	$1,665	$1,387
REF #: 8187916/60 02P, MENS LARGE QUARTZ, 18K GOLD LINK BRACELET	$15,500	$8,520	$5,425	$4,650	$3,875
REF #: 890910/60 99PP, LADIES QUARTZ, 18K GOLD LINK BRACELET, DIAMOND BEZEL, MOTHER OF PEARL DIAMOND DIAL	$14,250	$7,837	$4,987	$4,275	$3,562
REF #: 188901/60 02P, LADIES QUARTZ, STEEL AND 18K GOLD LINK BRACELET	$2,750	$1,512	$962	$825	$687
REF #: 188902/60 02C, MENS QUARTZ, STEEL AND 18K GOLD CAPPED LINK BRACELET	$3,950	$2,172	$1,382	$987	$987

PERPETUAL CALENDAR

	RETAIL	WHOLESALE	DUMP PRICES		
			EXCELLENT	GOOD	FAIR
REF #: 8136901/6012P, AUTOMATIC, 18K GOLD LINK BRACELET, MOON-PHASE MOVEMENT	$36,500	$20,075	$12,775	$10,950	$9,125

LE MODULOR

	RETAIL	WHOLESALE	DUMP PRICES		
			EXCELLENT	GOOD	FAIR
REF #: 8137241/3562D, AUTOMATIC-CHRONOMETER, 18K GOLD STRAP	$8,520	$4,686	$2,982	$2,556	$2,130
REF #: 9137241/6002P, AUTOMATIC-CHRONOMETER, STAINLESS STEEL	$3,750	$2,062	$1,312	$1,125	$937
REF #: 1137241/6061C, AUTOMATIC-CHRONOMETER, STEEL AND GOLD CAPPED LINK BRACELET	$5,800	$3,190	$2,030	$1,740	$1,450

VOYAGER

	RETAIL	WHOLESALE	DUMP PRICES		
			EXCELLENT	GOOD	FAIR
REF #: 8124/3525D, AUTOMATIC, 18K GOLD STRAP	$9,750	$5,362	$3,412	$2,925	$2,437
REF #: 9124913/3565DLT, AUTOMATIC, STEEL STRAP	$3,100	$1,705	$1,085	$930	$775

Audemars Piguet
20W 33rd Street Fourth Floor
New York, NY 10001-3305
(212) 594-3322

ROYAL OAK

	RETAIL	WHOLESALE	DUMP PRICES		
			EXCELLENT	GOOD	FAIR
ST 14800 0 0129/01,	$6,800	$3,740	$2,380	$2,040	$1,700
AUTOMATICMOVEMENT, DATE, SECOND HAND, STRAP, STAINLESS STEEL					
BA 14800 0 0009/01, AUTOMATIC	$14,300	$7,865	$5,005	$4,290	$3,575
MOVEMENT, DATE, SECOND HAND, STRAP, 18K GOLD					
ST 14790 0 0189/01,	$8,000	$4,400	$2,800	$2,400	$2,000
AUTOMATIC MOVEMENT, DATE, SECOND HAND, STAINLESS STEEL					
SA 15000 0 0789/01,	$11,900	$6,545	$4,165	$3,570	$2,975
AUTOMATIC MOVEMENT, DATE, SECOND HAND, TWO-TONE					
TR 14790 0 0789/01,	$15,200	$8,360	$6,688	$5,852	$4,180
AUTOMATIC MOVEMENT, DATE, SECOND HAND, TANTALUM ANDROSE GOLD					
BA 14790 0 0789/02,	$26,700	$14,685	$9,345	$8,010	$6,675
AUTOMATIC MOVEMENT, DATE, SECOND HAND, 18K GOLD					

ROYAL OAK DAY DATE

	RETAIL	WHOLESALE	DUMP PRICES		
			EXCELLENT	GOOD	FAIR
BA 25594 0 0789/01,	$31,200	$17,160	$10,920	$9,360	$7,800
AUTOMATIC MOVEMENT, DAY, DATE, GOLD, MOON PHASE					
ST 25594 0 0789/01,	$11,000	$6,050	$3,850	$3,300	$2,750
AUTOMATIC MOVEMENT, DAY, DATE, MOON PHASE, STAINLESS STEEL					

ROYAL OAK DUAL TIME

			DUMP PRICES		
	RETAIL	WHOLESALE	EXCELLENT	GOOD	FAIR
SA 25730 0 0789/01, AUTOMATIC MOVEMENT, DUAL TIME, TWO-TONE	$14,600	$8,030	$5,110	$4,380	$3,650
ST 25730 0 0789/01, AUTOMATIC MOVEMENT, DUAL TIME, STAINLESS STEEL	$12,600	$6,930	$4,410	$3,780	$3,150

ROYAL OAK PERPETUAL CALENDAR

			DUMP PRICES		
	RETAIL	WHOLESALE	EXCELLENT	GOOD	FAIR
BA 25654 0 0944/01, AUTOMATIC MOVEMENT, GOLD	$55,400	$30,470	$19,390	$16,620	$13,850
ST 25686 0 0944/02, AUTOMATIC MOVEMENT, STAINLESS STEEL	$40,000	$22,000	$14,000	$12,000	$10,000

LADIES ROYAL OAK

			DUMP PRICES		
	RETAIL	WHOLESALE	EXCELLENT	GOOD	FAIR
BA 668 00 0059/01, QUARTZ MOVEMENT, DATE, STRAP, GOLD	$8,250	$4,537	$2,887	$2,475	$2,062
SA 662 70 00722/01, QUARTZ MOVEMENT, DATE, TWO-TONE	$8,600	$4,750	$3,010	$2,580	$2,150
SP 662 70 00722/01, QUARTZ MOVEMENT, DATE, STAINLESS STEEL	$6,800	$3,740	$2,380	$2,040	$1,700
BA 662 70 00722/05, QUARTZ MOVEMENT, DATE, GOLD	$20,800	$11,440	$7,280	$6,240	$5,200

Breguet
201 RT 17W Eighth Floor
Rutherford, NJ 07070
(201) 507-4400

	RETAIL	WHOLESALE	DUMP PRICES EXCELLENT	GOOD	FAIR
3400SA/12/X90, GENTS MARINE STEEL AND 18K	$13,500	$7,425	$5,400	$4,725	$4,050
3400BA/12/196, GENTS MARINE 18K WITH STRAP	$17,000	$9,350	$6,800	$5,950	$5,100
3400BA/12/A90, GENTS MARINE 18K WITH BRACELET	$29,500	$16,225	$11,800	$10,325	$8,850
3460SA/12/X90, GENTS MARINE CHRONOGRAPH STEEL AND 18K	$21,500	$11,825	$8,600	$7,525	$6,450
3460PT/12/196, GENTS MARINE CHRONOGRAPH PLATINUM WITH STRAP	$36,000	$19,800	$14,850	$12,600	$10,800
3460BA/12/196, GENTS MARINE CHRONOGRAPH 18K BRACELET	$24,000	$13,200	$9,600	$8,400	$7,200
8400SA/12/X40, LADIES MARINE STEEL AND 18K BRACELET	$11,500	$6,325	$4,600	$4,025	$3,450
8400BA/12/141, LADIES MARINE 18K WITH STRAP	$13,500	$7,425	$5,400	$4,725	$4,050
8400BA/12/A40, LADIES MARINE 18K BRACELET	$23,500	$12,925	$9,400	$8,225	$7,050
3500BA/11/286, ULTRA THIN MANUAL, 18K WITH STRAP	$13,000	$7,150	$5,200	$4,550	$3,900
3210BA/29/264, MID SIZE MANUAL, 18K WITH STRAP	$8,950	$4,922	$3,580	$3,132	$2,685
3290BA/12/286, FULL SIZE MANUAL, 18K WITH STRAP	$11,000	$6,050	$4,400	$3,850	$3,300
3320BA/12/286, AUTOMATIC, 18K WITH STRAP	$15,000	$8,250	$6,000	$5,250	$4,500

Patek Philippe
1 Rockefeller Plaza #930
New York, NY 10020-2001
(212) 581-0870

CALATRAVA

	RETAIL	WHOLESALE	DUMP PRICES		
			EXCELLENT	GOOD	FAIR
3919, MENS MANUALLY WRIST WATCH, 18K/STRAP	$8,850	$4,867	$3,540	$3,097	$2,655
4809, LADIES MANUALLY WRIST WATCH, 18K/STRAP	$6,950	$3,822	$2,780	$2,432	$2,085
3919/8, MENS MANUALLY WRIST WATCH, 18K BRACELET	$17,800	$9,790	$7,120	$6,230	$5,340
4809/2, LADIES MANUALLY WRIST WATCH, 18K BRACELET	$15,300	$8,415	$6,120	$5,355	$4,540

GOLDEN ELLIPSE

	RETAIL	WHOLESALE	DUMP PRICES		
			EXCELLENT	GOOD	FAIR
3738/100, MENS ULTRA-THIN, SELF-WINDING MOVEMENT, 18K STRAP	$10,700	$5,885	$4,280	$3,745	$3,210
4826, LADIES MANUALLY WRIST WATCH, 18K STRAP	$7,200	$3,960	$2,880	$2,520	$2,160
3738/122, MENS ULTRA-THIN, SELF-WINDING MOVEMENT, 18K BRACELET	$22,300	$12,265	$8,920	$7,805	$6,690
4826/22, LADIES MANUALLY WRIST WATCH, 18K STRAP	$15,900	$8,745	$6,360	$5,565	$4,770
4830, LADIES QUARTZ MOVEMENT, 18K STRAP	$8,500	$4,675	$3,400	$2,975	$2,550
4830/1, LADIES QUARTZ MOVEMENT, 18 /BRACELET	$1,700	$935	$680	$595	$520

NAUTILUS

	RETAIL	WHOLESALE	DUMP PRICES		
			EXCELLENT	GOOD	FAIR
3800/1, MENS SELF-WINDING, DATE, 18K BRACELET	$28,000	$15,400	$11,200	$9,800	$8,400
3800/1A, MENS SELF-WINDING, DATE, STAINLESS STEEL BRACELET	$9,400	$5,170	$3,760	$3,290	$2,820
3800/1JA, MENS SELF-WINDING, DATE, TWO-TONE BRACELET	$17,000	$9,350	$6,800	$5,950	$5,100
4700/61JA, LADIES QUARTZ MOVEMENT, DATE, TWO-TONE BRACELET	$11,400	$6,270	$4,560	$3,990	$3,420
3900/1A, MENS QUARTZ MOVEMENT, DATE, STAINLESS STEEL BRACELET	$7,900	$4,345	$3,160	$2,765	$2,370
4700/51, LADIES QUARTZ MOVEMENT, DATE, 18K BRACELET	$17,800	$9,790	$7,120	$6,230	$5,340

202

NEPTUNE

	RETAIL	WHOLESALE	DUMP PRICES EXCELLENT	GOOD	FAIR
5081/1, MENS SELF-WINDING MOVEMENT, 18K, DATE, BRACELET	$12,800	$7,040	$5,120	$4,480	$3,840
4881/1, LADIES QUARTZ MOVEMENT, 18K, DATE, BRACELET	$15,900	$8,745	$6,360	$5,565	$4,770
4880/1A, LADIES QUARTZ MOVEMENT, STAINLESS STEEL, DATE, BRACELET	$6,500	$3,575	$2,600	$2,275	$1,950
4880/1JA, LADIES QUARTZ MOVEMENT, TWO-TONE, DATE, BRACELET	$8,750	$4,812	$3,500	$3,062	$2,625
5080/1JA, MENS SELF-WINDING, TWO-TONE, DATE, BRACELET	$12,800	$7,040	$5,120	$4,480	$3,840
5060, MENS SELF-WINDING, 18K, DATE, STRAP	$13,250	$7,287	$5,300	$4,637	$3,975
5080/1A, MENS SELF-WINDING MOVEMENT, STAINLESS STEEL, DATE, BRACELET	$7,950	$4,372	$3,180	$2,782	$2,385
5080/1A, MENS SELF-WINDING MOVEMENT, ANNUAL CALENDAR, 18K STRAP	$17,500	$9,625	$7,000	$6,125	$5,250

Vancheron Constantin
20 W 55th Street 12th Floor
New York, NY 10019
(212) 713-0707

LADIES STAINLESS STEEL OVERSEAS

			DUMP PRICES		
	RETAIL	WHOLESALE	EXCELLENT	GOOD	FAIR
12050/423A-7, AUTOMATIC	$7,500	$4,125	$2,625	$2,250	$1,875
12550/423A-7, AUTOMATIC WITH .33CT DIAMOND BEZEL	$10,900	$5,995	$3,815	$3,270	$2,725
16050/423A-7, QUARTZ	$5,500	$3,025	$1,925	$1,650	$1,375
16550/423A-7, QUARTZ WITH .33CT DIAMOND BEZEL	$8,900	$4,895	$3,115	$3,115	$2,225

LADIES 18K YELLOW GOLD OVERSEAS

			DUMP PRICES		
	RETAIL	WHOLESALE	EXCELLENT	GOOD	FAIR
12050/423J-7, AUTOMATIC	$20,000	$11,000	$7,000	$6,000	$5,000
12550/423J-7, AUTOMATIC WITH .33CT DIAMOND BEZEL	$23,000	$12,650	$8,050	$6,900	$5,750
16550/423J-7, QUARTZ WITH .33CT DIAMOND BEZEL	$21,500	$11,825	$7,525	$6,450	$5,375

MENS LARGE 37MM STAINLESS STEEL OVERSEAS

	RETAIL	WHOLESALE	DUMP PRICES		
			EXCELLENT	GOOD	FAIR
42040/423A-8, AUTOMATIC	$7,900	$4,345	$2,765	$2,370	$1,975
42540/423A-8, AUTOMATIC WITH .93CT DIAMOND BEZEL	$14,000	$7,700	$4,900	$4,200	$3,500
72040/423A-8, QUARTZ	$6,400	$3,520	$2,240	$1,920	$1,600
72540/423A-8, QUARTZ WITH .93CT DIAMOND BEZEL	$12,500	$6,875	$4,375	$3,750	$3,125

MENS 35MM STAINLESS STEEL OVERSEAS

	RETAIL	WHOLESALE	DUMP PRICES		
			EXCELLENT	GOOD	FAIR
42050/423A-8, AUTOMATIC	$7,700	$4,325	$2,695	$2,310	$1,925
42550/423A-8, AUTOMATIC WITH .76 DIAMOND BEZEL	$13,800	$7,590	$4,830	$4,140	$3,450
72050/423A-8, QUARTZ	$6,200	$3,410	$2,170	$1,860	$1,550
72550/423A-8, QUARTZ WITH .76CT DIAMOND BEZEL	$12,300	$6,765	$4,305	$3,690	$3,075

MENS LARGE 37MM 18K YELLOW GOLD OVERSEAS

	RETAIL	WHOLESALE	DUMP PRICES		
			EXCELLENT	GOOD	FAIR
42050/423J-8, AUTOMATIC	$26,000	$14,300	$9,100	$7,800	$6,500
42540/423J-8, AUTOMATIC WITH .93CT DIAMOND BEZEL	$32,500	$17,875	$11,375	$9,750	$8,125
72540/423J-8, QUARTZ WITH .93CT DIAMOND BEZEL	$31,000	$17,050	$10,850	$9,300	$7,750

MENS 35MM 18K YELLOW GOLD OVERSEAS

	RETAIL	WHOLESALE	DUMP PRICES		
			EXCELLENT	GOOD	FAIR
42050/423J-8, AUTOMATIC	$25,000	$13,750	$8,750	$7,500	$6,250
42550/423J-8, AUTOMATIC WITH .76CT DIAMOND BEZEL	$31,500	$17,325	$11,025	$9,450	$7,875
72550/423J-8, QUARTZ WITH .76CT DIAMOND BEZEL	$29,500	$16,225	$10,325	$8,850	$7,375
92239/000P, HISTORIQUE STRAP	$15,500	$8,525	$5,425	$4,650	$3,875
92012/000J, CROWN AT 12 STRAP	$19,900	$10,945	$6,965	$4,650	$4,975
47101/00P, HIST CHRONO STRAP	$27,000	$14,850	$9,450	$8,100	$6,750
49002/000J, 18K HIST CHRONO STRAP	$19,900	$10,945	$6,965	$5,970	$4,975
47050/00J, DAY, DATE, MOON STRAP	$18,900	$10,395	$6,965	$8,100	$6,750
11602/000J, LADIES SQUARE HISTORIQUE WITH DIAMOND BEZEL STRAP	$15,500	$8,525	$5,425	$4,650	$3,875
31100/000J, MENS SQUARE HISTORIQUE STRAP	$11,500	$6,325	$4,025	$3,450	$2,875
11100/464J, 18K LADIES SQUARE HISTORIQUE	$17,900	$9,845	$6,265	$5,370	$4,475
31602/464J, 18K MENS SQUARE HISTORIQUE WITH DIAMOND BEZEL	$24,500	$13,475	$8,575	$7,350	$6,125
92240/000J, ESSENTIELLE STRAP	$8,500	$4,675	$2,975	$2,550	$2,125
48100/00R, POWER RESERVE STRAP	$12,500	$6,875	$4,375	$3,750	$3,125
19001/00J, LADIES RECTANGULAR HISTORIQUE STRAP	$9,500	$5,225	$3,325	$2,850	$2,375
91501/000G, MENS RECTANGULAR HISTORIQUE STRAP	$9,900	$5,445	$3,465	$2,970	$2,475

MENS 35MM 18K YELLOW GOLD OVERSEAS (*CONTINUED*)

	RETAIL	WHOLESALE	DUMP PRICES		
			EXCELLENT	GOOD	FAIR
10002/000R, LADIES JALOUISE STRAP	$22,500	$12,375	$7,875	$6,750	$5,625
91002/00R, MENS JALOUISE STRAP	$25,900	$14,245	$9,065	$7,770	$6,475
10030/000J, LADIES MAGELLAN	$11,900	$6,545	$4,165	$3,570	$2,975
12020/967J, LADIES PHIDIAS 18K	$21,000	$11,550	$7,350	$6,300	$5,250
47020/967J, MENS PHIDIAS RC 18K	$23,500	$12,925	$8,225	$7,050	$5,875
49001/967J, PHIDIAS CHRONO 18K	$28,500	$15,675	$9,975	$8,550	$7,125
48200/967M, PHIDIAS GMT TWO-TONE	$12,900	$7,095	$4,515	$3,870	$3,225
47020/567M, PHIDIAS RC TWO-TONE	$11,500	$6,325	$4,025	$3,450	$2,875
12520/567M, LADIES PHIDIAS TWO-TONE	$14,500	$7,975	$5,075	$4,350	$3,625
43031/00J, PERPETUAL CAL	$43,500	$23,925	$15,225	$13,050	$10,875
43032/00P, SKEL PERP CAL	$87,500	$48,125	$30,625	$26,250	$21,875
49005/000R, PREP CAL: CHRONO STRAP	$57,500	$31,625	$20,125	$17,250	$14,375

Breitling USA Inc.
PO Box 110215
Stanford, CT 06911-0215
(203) 327-1411

OLD NAVITMER

	RETAIL	WHOLESALE	DUMP PRICES		
			EXCELLENT	GOOD	FAIR
301 SELF-WINDING CHRONO, STEEL CASE, BLACK DIAL, SILVER SUBDIALS, LEATHER STRAP, TANG-TYPE BUCKLE	$2,925	$1,608	$1,170	$1,023	$877
302 SELF-WINDING CHRONO, STEEL CASE, BLUE DIAL, SILVER SUBDIALS, NAVITIMER BRACELET IN STEEL	$3,775	$2,076	$1,510	$1,321	$1,321
303 SELF-WINDING CHRONO, STEEL AND 18K GOLD CASE, SILVER DIAL, GOLDEN SUBDIALS, LEATHER STRAP, TANG-TYPE BUCKLE	$3,325	$1,828	$1,330	$1,163	$997
304 SELF-WINDING CHRONO, 18K GOLD CASE, BLACK DIAL, SILVER SUBDIALS, PILOT BRACELET IN 18K GOLD	$18,400	$10,120	$7,360	$6,440	$5,520

COSMONAUTE

	RETAIL	WHOLESALE	DUMP PRICES		
			EXCELLENT	GOOD	FAIR
305 MECHANICAL CHRONO, STEEL CASE, BLACK DIAL, SILVER SUBDIALS, LEATHER STRAP, TANG-TYPE BUCKLE	$2,925	$1,608	$1,170	$1,023	$877
306 MECHANICAL CHRONO, STEEL AND 18K GOLD CASE, BLACK DIAL, SILVER SUBDIALS, LEATHER STRAP, TANG-TYPE BUCKLE	$3,325	$1,828	$1,330	$1,163	$997
307 MECHANICAL CHRONO, STEEL AND 18K GOLD CASE, SILVER DIAL, GOLDEN SUBDIALS, CROCO STRAP, 18K GOLD TANG-TYPE BUCKLE	$5,000	$2,750	$2,000	$1,750	$1,500
308 MECHANICAL CHRONO, 18K GOLD CASE, BLUE DIAL, SILVER SUBDIALS, CROCO STRAP, 18K TANG-TYPE BUCKLE	$9,250	$5,087	$3,700	$3,237	$2,775

AIRBORNE

	RETAIL	WHOLESALE	DUMP PRICES		
			EXCELLENT	GOOD	FAIR
309 SELF-WINDING CHRONO, STEEL CASE, BLACK DIAL, SILVER SUBDIALS, LEATHER STRAP, TANG-TYPE BUCKLE	$3,625	$1,993	$1,450	$1,268	$1,087
310 SELF-WINDING CHRONO, STEEL CASE, BLUE DIAL, SILVER SUBDIALS, NAVITIMER BRACELET IN STEEL	$4,475	$2,461	$1,790	$1,566	$1,342
311 SELF-WINDING CHRONO, 18K GOLD CASE, BLACK DIAL, SILVER SUBDIALS, CROCO STRAP, 18K GOLD TANG-TYPE BUCKLE	$8,250	$4,537	$3,300	$2,887	$2,475
312 SELF-WINDING CHRONO, STEEL AND 18K GOLD CASE, BLUE DIAL, SILVER SUBDIALS, SHARK STRAP, FOLDING CLASP	$4,250	$2,337	$1,700	$1,487	$1,275

LIMITED EDITION NAVITIMER

	RETAIL	WHOLESALE	DUMP PRICES		
			EXCELLENT	GOOD	FAIR
313 NAVITIMER 92 TOP GUN, SELF-WINDING CHRONO, STEEL AND 18K GOLD CASE, SILVER DIAL, GOLDEN SUBDIALS, LEATHER STRAP, TANG-TYPE STRAP	$3,275	$1,801	$1,310	$1,146	$982
314 COSMONAUTÈ, SCOTT CARPENTER, MECHANICAL CHRONO, STEEL CASE, BLACK DIAL, SILVER SUBDIALS, PILOT BRACELET IN STEEL	$3,925	$2,158	$1,570	$1,373	$1,177
315 MONTBRILLIANT BLUE ANGELS, SELF-WINDING CHRONO, 18K ROSE GOLD CASE, SILVER DIAL, CROCO STRAP, 18K ROSE GOLD TANG-TYPE BUCKLE	$9,275	$5,101	$3,710	$6,028	$2,782

AVIASTAR

	RETAIL	WHOLESALE	DUMP PRICES		
			EXCELLENT	GOOD	FAIR
316 SELF-WINDING CHRONO, STEEL CASE, BLACK DIAL, NAVITIMER BRACELET IN STEEL	$3,175	$1,746	$1,270	$1,111	$952
317 SELF-WINDING CHRONO, STEEL CASE, BLACK DIAL, LEATHER STRAP TANG-TYPE BUCKLE	$2,325	$1,278	$930	$813	$697

MONTBRILLIANT

	RETAIL	WHOLESALE	DUMP PRICES		
			EXCELLENT	GOOD	FAII
318 SELF-WINDING CHRONO, 18K ROSE GOLD CASE, SILVER DIAL, CROCO STRAP, 18K ROSE GOLD TANG-TYPE BUCKLE	$9,125	$5,018	$3,650	$3,193	$2,73
319 SELF-WINDING CHRONO, STEEL CASE, SILVER DIAL, NAVITIMER BRACELET IN STEEL	$3,975	$2,186	$1,749	$1,530	$1,093
320 SELF-WINDING CHRONO, 18K ROSE GOLD CASE, BLACK DIAL, NAVITIMER BRACELET IN 18K ROSE GOLD	$19,325	$10,628	$7,730	$6,763	$5,797
321 SELF-WINDING CHRONO, PLATINUM CASE, BLACK DIAL, CROCO STRAP, 18K WHITE GOLD TANG-TYPE BUCKLE	$17,225	$9,473	$6,890	$6,028	$5,167
322 SELF-WINDING CHRONO, STEEL CASE, BLACK DIAL, LEATHER STRAP, TANG-TYPE BUCKLE	$3,125	$1,718	$1,250	$1,093	$937

SPATIOGRAPHE

	RETAIL	WHOLESALE	DUMP PRICES		
			EXCELLENT	GOOD	FAIR
323 SELF-WINDING CHRONO, STEEL CASE, BLACK DIAL, CROCO STRAP, TANG-TYPE BUCKLE	$3,425	$1,883	$1,370	$1,198	$1,027
DITTO WITH LEATHER STRAP	$3,225	$1,773	$1,290	$1,128	$967
324 SELF-WINDING CHRONO, STEEL CASE, BLACK DIAL, NAVITIMER BRACELET IN STEEL	$4,075	$2,241	$1,630	$1,426	$1,222
325 SELF-WINDING CHRONO, 18K ROSE GOLD CASE, BLACK DIAL, CROCO STRAP, 18K ROSE GOLD TANG-TYPE BUCKLE	$10,225	$5,623	$4,090	$3,578	$3,067
326 SELF-WINDING CHRONO, PLATINUM CASE, BLACK DIAL, CROCO STRAP, 18K WHITE GOLD TANG-TYPE BUCKLE	$19,725	$10,848	$7,890	$6,903	$5,917

CHRONOMAT

	RETAIL	WHOLESALE	DUMP PRICES		
			EXCELLENT	GOOD	FAIR
331 SELF-WINDING CHRONO, STEEL CASE, RHODIUM DIAL, BLACK SUBDIALS, PILOT BRACELET IN STEEL	$3,675	$2,021	$1,470	$1,286	$1,102
332 SELF-WINDING CHRONO, STEEL CASE, BLACK DIAL, LEATHER STRAP, TANG-TYPE BUCKLE	$2,825	$1,553	$1,130	$988	$847
333 SELF-WINDING CHRONO, STEEL CASE, BLUE DIAL, SILVER SUBDIALS, SHARK STRAP, FOLDING CLASP	$3,050	$1,677	$1,220	$1,067	$915
334 SELF-WINDING CHRONO, STEEL CASE, SILVER DIAL, CROCO STRAP, TANG-TYPE BUCKLE	$3,025	$1,663	$1,210	$1,058	$907
335 SELF-WINDING CHRONO, TWO-TONE STEEL CASE, BLACK DIAL, GOLDEN SUBDIALS, LEATHER STRAP, TANG-TYPE BUCKLE	$3,025	$1,663	$1,210	$1,058	$907
336 SELF-WINDING CHRONO, TWO-TONE STEEL CASE, BURGUNDY DIAL, GOLDEN SUBDIALS, CROCO STRAP, TANG-TYPE BUCKLE	$3,225	$1,773	$1,290	$1,228	$967
337 SELF-WINDING CHRONO, TWO-TONE STEEL CASE, SILVER DIAL, SHARK STRAP, FOLDING CLASP	$3,250	$1,787	$1,300	$1,137	$975
338 SELF-WINDING CHRONO, TWO-TONE STEEL CASE, BLUE DIAL, GOLDEN SUBDIALS, LEATHER STRAP, TANG-TYPE BUCKLE	$3,025	$1,663	$1,210	$1,058	$907
339 SELF-WINDING CHRONO, TWO-TONE STEEL CASE, WHITE DIAL, TWO-TONE UTC MODULE, LEATHER STRAP, TANG-TYPE BUCKLE	$3,800	$2,090	$1,520	$1,330	$1,140

CHRONOMAT *(CONTINUED)*

	RETAIL	WHOLESALE	DUMP PRICES EXCELLENT	GOOD	FAIR
340 SELF-WINDING CHRONO, TWO-TONE STEEL CASE, SMOKE-GRAY DIAL, BLUE SUBDIALS, PILOT BRACELET IN STEEL	$3,875	$2,131	$1,550	$1,356	$1,162
341 SELF-WINDING CHRONO, TWO-TONE STEEL CASE, BLACK DIAL, PILOT BRACELET IN STEEL	$3,875	$2,131	$1,550	$1,356	$1,162
342 SELF-WINDING CHRONO, TWO-TONE STEEL CASE, BLUE DIAL, ROULEAUX BRACELET IN STEEL	$3,525	$1,938	$1,410	$1,233	$1,057
343 SELF-WINDING CHRONO, STEEL AND 18K GOLD CASE, BLUE DIAL, ROULEAUX BRACELET IN STEEL AND 18K GOLD	$4,575	$2,516	$1,830	$1,601	$1,372
344 SELF-WINDING CHRONO, STEEL AND 18K GOLD CASE, WHITE DIAL, SHARK STRAP, FOLDING CLASP	$3,750	$2,062	$1,500	$1,312	$1,125
345 SELF-WINDING CHRONO, STEEL AND 18K GOLD CASE, CHAMPAGNE DIAL, PILOT BRACELET IN STEEL AND 18K GOLD	$5,200	$2,860	$2,080	$1,820	$1,560
346 SELF-WINDING CHRONO, STEEL AND 18K GOLD CASE, GOLDEN SUBDIALS, LEATHER STRAP, TANG-TYPE BUCKLE	$3,525	$1,938	$1,410	$1,233	$1,057
347 SELF-WINDING CHRONO, 18K WHITE GOLD CASE, BLUE DIAL, 18K WHITE GOLD PILOT BRACELET	$25,400	$13,970	$10,160	$8,890	$7,620
348 SELF-WINDING CHRONO, 18K GOLD CASE, YELLOW DIAL, BLACK SUBDIALS, CROCO STRAP, 18K WHITE GOLD TANG-TYPE BUCKLE	$13,175	$7,246	$5,270	$4,611	$3,952

CHRONOMAT *(CONTINUED)*

	RETAIL	WHOLESALE	DUMP PRICES		
			EXCELLENT	GOOD	FAIR
349 SELF-WINDING CHRONO, 18K GOLD CASE, WHITE DIAL, CROCO STRAP, 18K GOLD TANG-TYPE BUCKLE	$10,750	$5,912	$4,300	$3,762	$3,225
350 SELF-WINDING CHRONO, 18K GOLD CASE, MOTHER OF PEARL DIAL, BLUE SUBDIALS, PILOT BRACELET IN 18K GOLD	$20,350	$11,192	$8,140	$7,122	$6,105
351 SELF-WINDING CHRONO, 18K GOLD CASE, BLACK DIAL, CROCO STRAP, 18K GOLD TANG-TYPE BUCKLE	$10,750	$5,912	$4,300	$3,762	$3,225
352 SELF-WINDING CHRONO, 18K GOLD CASE, BLUE DIAL, GOLDEN SUBDIALS, PILOT BRACELET IN 18K GOLD	$20,000	$11,000	$8,000	$7,000	$6,000

CHRONOMAT BLACKBIRD

	RETAIL	WHOLESALE	DUMP PRICES		
			EXCELLENT	GOOD	FAIR
353 SELF-WINDING CHRONO, STEEL CASE, BLACK DIAL, PILOT BRACELET IN STEEL	$3,675	$2,021	$1,470	$1,286	$1,102

CHRONOMAT LONGITUDE

	RETAIL	WHOLESALE	DUMP PRICES		
			EXCELLENT	GOOD	FAIR
354 SELF-WINDING CHRONO, STEEL CASE, WHITE DIAL, LEATHER STRAP, TANG-TYPE BUCKLE	$3,225	$1,773	$1,290	$1,128	$967
355 SELF-WINDING CHRONO, STEEL CASE, ANTHRACITE DIAL, CROCO STRAP, TANG-TYPE BUCKLE	$3,425	$1,883	$1,370	$1,198	$1,027
356 SELF-WINDING CHRONO, STEEL CASE, YELLOW DIAL, BLACK SUBDIALS, PILOT BRACELET IN STEEL	$4,075	$2,241	$1,630	$1,426	$1,222

CROSSWIND

	RETAIL	WHOLESALE	DUMP PRICES		
			EXCELLENT	GOOD	FAIR
357 SELF-WINDING CHRONO, 18K GOLD CASE, BLACK DIAL, CROCO STRAP, 18K GOLD TANG-TYPE BUCKLE	$11,725	$6,448	$4,690	$4,103	$3,517
358 SELF-WINDING CHRONO, 18K GOLD CASE, WHITE DIAL, CROCO STRAP, 18K GOLD TANG-TYPE BUCKLE	$11,725	$6,448	$4,690	$4,103	$3,517
359 SELF-WINDING CHRONO, 18K GOLD BLUE DIAL, PILOT BRACELET IN 18K GOLD	$20,975	$11,536	$8,390	$7,341	$6,292
360 SELF-WINDING CHRONO, STEEL CASE, BLACK DIAL, LEATHER STRAP, TANG-TYPE BUCKLE	$3,125	$1,718	$1,250	$1,093	$937
361 SELF-WINDING CHRONO, STEEL CASE, WHITE DIAL, CROCO STRAP, TANG-TYPE BUCKLE	$3,325	$1,828	$1,330	$1,163	$997
362 SELF-WINDING CHRONO, STEEL CASE, BLUE DIAL, PILOT BRACELET IN STEEL	$3,975	$2,186	$1,586	$1,391	$1,192
363 SELF-WINDING CHRONO, TWO-TONE STEEL CASE, BLACK DIAL, PILOT BRACELET IN STEEL	$4,175	$2,296	$1,670	$1,461	$1,252
364 SELF-WINDING CHRONO, TWO-TONE STEEL CASE, WHITE DIAL, LEATHER STRAP, TANG-TYPE BUCKLE	$3,325	$1,828	$1,330	$1,163	$997
365 SELF-WINDING CHRONO, TWO-TONE STEEL CASE, BLUE DIAL, SHARK STRAP, FOLDING CLASP	$3,550	$1,952	$1,420	$1,242	$1,065

CHRONO COCKPIT

	RETAIL	WHOLESALE	DUMP PRICES		
			EXCELLENT	GOOD	FAIR
366 SELF-WINDING CHRONO, STEEL CASE, BLUE DIAL, SILVER SUBDIALS, LEATHER STRAP, TANG-TYPE BUCKLE	$3,125	$1,718	$1,250	$1,093	$937
367 SELF-WINDING CHRONO, TWO-TONE STEEL CASE, WHITE DIAL, CROCO STRAP, TANG-TYPE BUCKLE	$3,525	$1,938	$1,410	$1,233	$1,057
368 SELF-WINDING CHRONO, TWO-TONE STEEL CASE, BLACK DIAL, GOLDEN SUBDIALS, LEATHER STRAP, TANG-TYPE BUCKLE	$3,325	$1,828	$1,330	$1,163	$997
369 SELF-WINDING CHRONO, TWO-TONE STEEL CASE, BLUE DIAL, GOLDEN SUBDIALS, ROULEAUX BRACELET IN STEEL	$3,825	$2,103	$1,530	$1,338	$1,147
370 SELF-WINDING CHRONO, TWO-TONE STEEL CASE, BLUE DIAL, PILOT BRACELET IN STEEL	$4,175	$2,296	$1,670	$1,461	$1,252
371 SELF-WINDING CHRONO, STEEL AND 18K GOLD CASE, MOTHER OF PEARL DIAL, BLUE SUBDIALS, CROCO STRAP, TANG-TYPE BUCKLE	$4,375	$2,406	$1,750	$1,531	$1,312

WINGS AUTOMATIC

	RETAIL	WHOLESALE	DUMP PRICES		
			EXCELLENT	GOOD	FAIR
381 SELF-WINDING WATCH, 18K GOLD CASE, MOTHER OF PEARL DIAL, CROCO STRAP, 18K GOLD TANG-TYPE BUCKLE	$7,325	$4,028	$2,930	$2,563	$2,197
383 SELF-WINDING WATCH, STEEL CASE, BLUE DIAL, LEATHER STRAP, TANG-TYPE BUCKLE	$1,725	$948	$690	$603	$517
384 SELF-WINDING WATCH, TWO-TONE STEEL CASE, SILVER DIAL, SHARK STRAP FOLDING CLASP	$2,150	$1,182	$860	$752	$645
DITTO WITH LEATHER STRAP	$1,925	$1,058	$770	$673	$577
385 SELF-WINDING WATCH, TWO-TONE STEEL CASE, BLACK DIAL, ROULEAUX BRACELET IN STEEL AND 18K GOLD	$2,975	$1,636	$1,190	$1,041	$892
386 SELF-WINDING WATCH, STEEL CASE, SLATE-GRAY DIAL, PILOT BRACELET IN STEEL	$2,575	$1,416	$1,030	$901	$772

WINGS QUARTZ

	RETAIL	WHOLESALE	DUMP PRICES		
			EXCELLENT	GOOD	FAIR
387 QUARTZ, STEEL CASE, WHITE DIAL LEATHER STRAP, TANG-TYPE BUCKLE	$1,525	$838	$610	$533	$457
388 QUARTZ, STEEL CASE, BLACK DIAL, ROULEAUX BRACELET IN STEEL	$2,025	$1,113	$810	$708	$607
389 QUARTZ, TWO-TONE STEEL CASE, WHITE DIAL, SHARK STRAP, FOLDING CLASP	$1,950	$1,072	$780	$682	$585
390 QUARTZ WATCH, TWO-TONE STEEL CASE, BLUE DIAL, PILOT BRACELET IN STEEL	$2,575	$1,416	$1,030	$901	$772
DITTO WITH LEATHER STRAP	$1,725	$948	$690	$603	$517

CALLISTO

	RETAIL	WHOLESALE	DUMP PRICES		
			EXCELLENT	GOOD	FAIR
399 QUARTZ, STEEL CASE, BLACK DIAL, LEATHER STRAP, TANG-TYPE BUCKLE	$1,475	$811	$590	$516	$442
400 QUARTZ, TWO-TONE STEEL CASE, WHITE DIAL, CROCO STRAP, TANG-TYPE BUCKLE	$1,875	$1,031	$750	$656	$562
401 QUARTZ, STEEL CASE, BLUE DIAL, PILOT BRACELET IN STEEL	$2,325	$1,278	$930	$813	$697
402 QUARTZ, STEEL CASE, SILVER DIAL SHARK STRAP, FOLDING CLASP	$1,700	$935	$680	$595	$595
403 QUARTZ, TWO-TONE STEEL CASE, BLACK DIAL, PILOT BRACELET IN STEEL	$2,525	$1,388	$1,010	$883	$757
404 QUARTZ, TWO-TONE STEEL CASE, BLUE DIAL, LEATHER STRAP, TANG-TYPE BUCKLE	$1,675	$921	$670	$586	$502
405 QUARTZ, TWO-TONE STEEL CASE, BLUE DIAL, ROULEAUX BRACELET IN STEEL AND 18K GOLD	$2,725	$1,498	$1,090	$953	$817

AEROSPACE

	RETAIL	WHOLESALE	DUMP PRICES		
			EXCELLENT	GOOD	FAIR
427 QUARTZ CHRONO, TITANIUM CASE, BLACK DIAL, LEATHER STRAP TANG-TYPE BUCKLE	$1,825	$1,003	$730	$638	$547
428 QUARTZ CHRONO, TITANIUM CASE, BLUE DIAL, PROFESSIONAL BRACELET IN TITANIUM	$2,200	$1,210	$880	$770	$660
429 QUARTZ CHRONO, TITANIUM CASE, TITANIUM DIAL, TITANIUM UTC MODULE, AEROSPACE BRACELET IN TITANIUM	$2,725	$1,498	$1,090	$953	$817
430 QUARTZ CHRONO, TWO-TONE TITANIUM CASE, BLACK DIAL, TWO-TONE TITANIUM UTC MODULE, DIVER STRAP, TANG-TYPE BUCKLE	$2,700	$1,485	$1,080	$945	$810
431 QUARTZ CHRONO, TWO-TONE TITANIUM CASE, BLUE DIAL, AEROSPACE BRACELET IN TWO-TONE TITANIUM	$2,150	$1,182	$860	$752	$645
432 QUARTZ CHRONO, TWO-TONE TITANIUM CASE, GREENISH-GRAY DIAL, PROFESSIONAL BRACELET IN TITANIUM	$2,300	$1,265	$920	$805	$690
433 QUARTZ CHRONO, 18K GOLD CASE, BLACK DIAL, CROCO STRAP, 18K GOLD TANG-TYPE BUCKLE	$9,725	$5,348	$3,890	$3,403	$2,917
434 QUARTZ CHRONO, 18K GOLD CASE, BLUE DIAL, PROFESSIONAL BRACELET IN 18K GOLD	$17,975	$9,886	$7,190	$6,291	$5,392
435 QUARTZ CHRONO, 18K WHITE GOLD CASE, YELLOW DIAL, PROFESSIONAL BRACELET IN 18K WHITE GOLD	$25,450	$13,997	$10,180	$8,907	$7,635

CHRONOSPACE

	RETAIL	WHOLESALE	DUMP PRICES		
			EXCELLENT	GOOD	FAIR
436 QUARTZ CHRONO, STEEL CASE. BLUE DIAL, DIVER STRAP, TANG-TYPE BUCKLE	$1,225	$673	$490	$428	$367
437 QUARTZ CHRONO, STEEL CASE, BLUE DIAL, PROFESSIONAL BRACELET IN STEEL	$1,325	$728	$530	$463	$397
438 QUARTZ CHRONO, STEEL CASE, ANTHRACITE DIAL, UTC MODULE STEEL, SHARK STRAP, FOLDING CLASP	$2,175	$1,196	$870	$761	$652

JUPITER PILOT

	RETAIL	WHOLESALE	DUMP PRICES		
			EXCELLENT	GOOD	FAIR
439 QUARTZ CHRONO, STEEL CASE, BLACK DIAL, SILVER SUBDIALS, JUPITER BRACELET IN STEEL	$1,425	$783	$570	$498	$427
440 QUARTZ CHRONO, STEEL CASE, SILVER DIAL, BLACK SUBDIALS, DIVER STRAP, TANG-TYPE BUCKLE	$1,225	$673	$490	$428	$367
441 QUARTZ CHRONO, STEEL CASE, BLUE DIAL, SILVER SUBDIALS, SHARK STRAP, FOLDING CLASP	$1,450	$797	$580	$507	$435
442 QUARTZ CHRONO, STEEL CASE, ANTHRACITE DIAL, LEATHER STRAP, TANG-TYPE BUCKLE	$1,025	$563	$410	$358	$307
443 QUARTZ CHRONO, STEEL CASE, SILVER DIAL, SHARK STRAP, FOLDING CLASP	$1,250	$687	$500	$437	$375
444 QUARTZ CHRONO, STEEL CASE, BLUE DIAL, PROFESSIONAL BRACELET IN STEEL	$1,125	$618	$450	$393	$337

CHRONO COLT AUTOMATIC

	RETAIL	WHOLESALE	DUMP PRICES		
			EXCELLENT	GOOD	FAIR
445 SELF-WINDING CHRONO, STEEL CASE, BLACK DIAL, SILVER SUBDIALS, PROFESSIONAL BRACELET IN STEEL	$2,200	$1,210	$880	$770	$660
446 SELF-WINDING CHRONO, STEEL CASE, WHITE DIAL, BLACK SUBDIALS, DIVER STRAP, TANG-TYPE BUCKLE	$2,100	$1,155	$840	$735	$630
447 SELF-WINDING CHRONO, STEEL CASE, BLUE DIAL, SILVER SUBDIALS, SHARK STRAP, FOLDING CLASP	$2,325	$1,278	$930	$813	$697

CHRONO COLT QUARTZ

	RETAIL	WHOLESALE	DUMP PRICES		
			EXCELLENT	GOOD	FAIR
448 QUARTZ CHRONO, STEEL CASE, BLACK DIAL, SILVER SUBDIALS, PROFESSIONAL BRACELET IN STEEL	$1,425	$783	$570	$498	$427
449 QUARTZ CHRONO, STEEL CASE, BLUE DIAL, BLACK SUBDIALS, DIVER STRAP, TANG-TYPE BUCKLE	$1,325	$728	$570	$463	$397
450 QUARTZ CHRONO, STEEL CASE, SILVER DIAL, BLACK SUBDIALS SHARK STRAP, FOLDING CLASP	$1,550	$852	$620	$525	$465

225

CHRONO COLT TRANSOCEAN

	RETAIL	WHOLESALE	DUMP PRICES		
			EXCELLENT	GOOD	FAIR
451 QUARTZ CHRONO, STEEL CASE, ANTHRACITE DIAL, PROFESSIONAL BRACELET IN STEEL	$1,625	$893	$650	$560	$487
452 QUARTZ CHRONO, STEEL CASE, SILVER DIAL, BLUE SUBDIALS, SHARK STRAP, FOLDING CLASP	$1,750	$962	$700	$612	$525

COLT AUTOMATIC

	RETAIL	WHOLESALE	DUMP PRICES		
			EXCELLENT	GOOD	FAIR
453 SELF-WINDING WATCH, STEEL CASE, WHITE DIAL, DIVER STRAP, TANG-TYPE BUCKLE	$975	$536	$390	$341	$292
454 SELF-WINDING WATCH, STEEL CASE, GREENISH-GRAY DIAL, PROFESSIONAL BRACELET IN STEEL	$1,075	$591	$430	$376	$322

COLT QUARTZ

	RETAIL	WHOLESALE	DUMP PRICES		
			EXCELLENT	GOOD	FAIR
455 QUARTZ, STEEL CASE, BLUE DIAL, DIVER STRAP, TANG-TYPE BUCKLE	$850	$467	$340	$297	$255
456 QUARTZ, STEEL CASE, RHODIUM DIAL, PROFESSIONAL BRACELET IN STEEL	$950	$522	$380	$365	$285

COLT SUPEROCEAN

	RETAIL	WHOLESALE	DUMP PRICES		
			EXCELLENT	GOOD	FAIR
457 SELF-WINDING, 18K GOLD CASE, BLACK DIAL, PROFESSIONAL BRACELET IN 18K GOLD	$17,500	$9,625	$7,000	$6,125	$5,250
458 SELF-WINDING, STEEL CASE, BLUE DIAL, DIVER STRAP, TANG-TYPE BUCKLE	$1,625	$893	$650	$568	$487
459 SELF-WINDING, STEEL CASE, BLACK DIAL, PROFESSIONAL BRACELET IN STEEL	$1,725	$948	$690	$603	$517

20 COLLECTIBLE WATCHES

PATEK PHILIPPE POCKET WATCHES	LOW	HIGH
MINUTE REPEATERS, 18K	$6,000	$12,000
PERPETUAL CALENDAR, 18K	$10,000	$20,000
PERPETUAL CALENDAR WITH CHRONOGRAPH AND MINUTE-REPEATING COMPLICATION, 18K	$35,000	$75,000
PATEK PHILIPPE WRIST WATCHES		
PERPETUAL CALENDAR, 18K	$15,000	$50,000
PERPETUAL CALENDAR WITH CHRONOGRAPH, 18K	$30,000	$100,000
CHRONOGRAPH, 18K	$12,000	$50,000
MINUTE REPEATER, 18K	$100,000	$300,000
PLATINUM	$150,000	$500,000
WORLD TIME, 18K	$30,000	$250,000
BREGUET WRIST WATCHES		
MOON PHASE WITH POWER RESERVE	$9,000	$12,000
TOURBILLION	$30,000	$50,000
ROLEX WRIST WATCH		
STEEL BUBBLE BACK	$500	$1,500
14K BUBBLE BACK	$1,500	$3,000
18K BUBBLE BACK	$2,000	$4,000
STEEL DAYTONA	$3,000	$6,000
18K DAYTONA	$9,000	$14,000
STEEL PRINCE	$2,500	$3,500
14K PRINCE	$3,500	$5,500
18K PRINCE	$6,000	$10,000
18K DAY, DATE, MOON PHASE	$7,000	$20,000

Fred's Complete Guide to Sorting and Cleaning Jewelry

After completing your Treasure Hunt, you have a pile of jewelry, and the first thing you need to do is sort it by type. Make five smaller piles:

1. Diamond jewelry

2. Diamond and colored-stone jewelry

3. Colored-stone jewelry

4. Gold jewelry

5. Costume and silver jewelry

Next, there are two ways we can clean our jewelry, manually and electronically. Let's talk about the manual method first. We're going to need a few things from the supermarket:

1. Parsons Sudsing Ammonia

2. Plastic food containers (4) (Tupperware is fine)

3. Dishwashing liquid (I use Dawn)

4. One toothbrush, firm

5. Lint-free cloths

Okay, we've done our shopping, and we're back at the kitchen table with the goods. Let's get started. Here's how we *manually* clean our jewelry, by category.

Diamond Jewelry

- In a plastic container, mix one part Parsons Sudsing Ammonia with eight parts of water.

- Place the diamond jewelry into the solution. (It's fine if pieces lie on top of one another—just don't bang them together.)

- Let the jewelry soak for an hour or two, or longer if it's really dirty. Don't worry about leaving it in too long—the solution won't harm the jewelry.

- After soaking, pick out each piece of jewelry and scrub it with the toothbrush until it gets foamy. (This is the new toothbrush, not the one you use for your teeth.)

- After making sure your sink drain is plugged, either with a rubber stopper or by pulling the mechanical stopper, rinse the jewelry under cool water. The reason for stopping the drain is that sometimes, with an old piece of jewelry, all that is holding the stones in is the dirt, and the stones may fall out.

If they do, place them in a zip-lock plastic bag for transport to the appraiser.

- Dry the jewelry with the lint-free cloth, inspecting it carefully to check for caked-on dirt between the prongs or in gaps and crevices in the mounting. If any dirt remains, repeat the process.

If you're thinking, "Man! What a hassle this is!" remember that the appraiser won't be able to determine the true value of the jewelry unless it's good and clean, and the true value is what we're after. If we don't find that, we'll never make any money in this business.

Diamond and Colored Stone Jewelry and Colored Stone Jewelry

These categories use the same solution, but give each category its own container. You've gone to the trouble of sorting the stuff out, so you might as well keep them separate.

- In each plastic container, mix one tablespoon of dishwashing liquid with one cup (8 oz.) of water. If the solution isn't deep enough to completely cover all the jewelry in the container, double the recipe.

- Let the jewelry soak for an hour or two.

- Scrub lightly with the toothbrush.

- Rinse (stopper that drain!).

- Dry with the lint-free cloth.

- Examine for dirt, and repeat if necessary.

Gold Jewelry

Gold is evaluated strictly by weight and purity, so don't worry about removing scratches or tarnish. It's not appraised under a loupe or a microscope, but on a scale.

Costume Jewelry and Silver

How do I put this diplomatically? Oh, what the heck: It's junk. It has no real value, and we're not going to get it appraised.

• However, if you're not *sure* it's costume jewelry, create another category and call it "Mystery Pile." When you go to the appraiser, tell him you don't want him to appraise the fakes, and would he please separate the fakes from the real thing without charge. A good appraiser can tell at a glance and should not charge you for that.

The second process for cleaning our jewelry is *electronically*, with an ultrasonic cleaner. The only difference is that the ultrasonic device takes the place of the plastic container. The cleaner can be purchased at your local department store for about $25 to $50. The advantage to the electronic cleaner is that it tends to do the job better and faster than manual cleaning.

• Follow the same instructions as before for mixing the cleaning solutions, and pour in enough solution to reach the "fill" line.

• Turn the machine on "High," and let it run for thirty minutes to an hour.

• Remove the jewelry, and scrub, rinse, and dry as in the manual process. Repeat if necessary.

TOOLS OF THE TRADE

Throughout this book I've referred to various pieces of equipment such as loupes, master sets, and leverage gauges. Getting into the diamond business is just like going off to school with your new pencils, notebooks, rulers, and calculators. There are some basic tools that make your job easier and make you more professional. After all, I've gotten you into the boat—I might as well give you a paddle!

I've grouped the equipment according to your level of involvement: One-Timer, Part-Timer, or Major Leaguer. Look at it this way: If you're only going to play golf once, you don't need to buy a set of clubs. If you plan to play once in a while, maybe you'll get a putter and a pair of shoes. And if you're aiming for the PGA tour, you'll get the full set, and the best you can afford.

I've also given you the names of a couple of good suppliers you can call to get everything you need.

One-Timers—You're only doing this once, as your nickname clearly indicates. You can get by using the appraiser's equipment. Don't buy a thing.

Part-Timers—You should purchase the basic outfit:

Loupe	This is a must-have, like a navy blue blazer in a guy's basic wardrobe.

My recommendation: 10X Hand loupe, by Gem Instruments, order #310000. Features the largest-diameter (20.5mm) lens of any 10X loupe, and comes with its own attractive leather carrying pouch. The ultimate magnifying experience for the smart diamond buyer.

Leverage Gauge   A diamond buyer without a leverage gauge is like a sailor without a compass. It's the *only* tool for accurately measuring a diamond.

My recommendation: U.S. Leverage Gauge, from Gem Instruments, order #164000 Comes with an elegant felt-lined case, complete operating instructions, and a one-year warrantee.

Polishing Cloths   Nonabrasive, lint-free cloths that remove oil and dirt to allow for accurate color and clarity grading.

My recommendation: Ultra fine weave gem cloth from Gem Instruments, order #543000. It's what the pros use.

Stone Tweezers   The only correct way to pick up loose diamond stones is with tweezers. Perfect for gripping stones while you grade and measure.

My recommendation: Stainless steel chrome-finish tweezers, $6\frac{1}{4}$", Gem Instruments, order #524000.

Locking Tweezers These provide a self-locking mechanism that grips the stone for easier handling and measuring.

My recommendation: High-grade stainless steel, black finish, 5½", Gem Instruments, order #517000.

Plotting Papers Have little outline maps of the different gem shapes. Use them to plot a diamond's individual blemishes and inclusions for future identification.

My recommendation: Adhesive diamond labels, Kassoy, order #DIF20, DIF30.

Folding Trays White trays, for examining loose diamonds for color grade.

My recommendation: Ultrawhite prefolded cards for color grading.

Prong Pull Used to remove diamonds and other gem-stones from settings, so that they can be more accurately weighed and measured.

My recommendation: Quality Prong Lifter, Kassoy, order #53.144.

Parcel Papers These are the little folding papers that diamond dealers use to hold loose stones. Once a diamond is pulled from its setting, a parcel paper will protect it 'til it finds a new home.

My recommendation: Outside paper, white; inside paper, blue and white. Kassoy, order #61.0570.

Diamond Scale The only way to get the exact weight of a diamond is to weigh it on a diamond scale.

My recommendation: Dendrites Gemscale 100, Gem Instruments, order #100051.

Master Set (Optional) The only way to determine the color grade of an unknown diamond is to compare it with a known color. If you'd like to try this yourself, without the appraiser's assistance, buy your own master set. You have two options, a diamond master set or a cubic zirconia master set.

My recommendation: Start with a CZ master set, which is only a few hundred dollars versus a few thousand for a genuine diamond master set. Over time, though, the CZ's begin to discolor. By then you should be able to afford the diamond master set! Kassoy, order #DC1010.

Major Leaguers—Go for the good stuff as soon as you can afford it. This equipment is very expensive, so you may want to hold off purchasing these items until you've "Done the Donald" a few times and have cash to spare.

Gem Microscope This has many advantages over a loupe. It has a zoom lens, locking tweezers, top lighting, black-field illumination, and other handy features. This is a must for the serious diamond broker making the big bucks.

My recommendation: Gemolite Ultima B Mark X, from Gem Instruments, Order #805000.

Diamond Lite™ The best way to view your diamond is under cool, diffused, balanced white light. Perfect for back lighting to color grade and check for fluorescence.

My recommendation: Diamond Lite™ from Gem Instruments, Order #180000.

Colorimeter Color grades loose and mounted diamonds in seconds. This powerful new development puts even difficult color calls at your fingertips.

My recommendation: Gran Colorimeter from Gem Instruments, order #283000.

Diamond Scale For the Major Leaguer, the serious scale, perfect for weighing individual stones or large quantities of diamonds or gold.

My recommendation: Mettler™ Jewelers Scale from Gem Instruments, order #100203.

Diamond Tester Real—or fake? This tells you for sure. Just press the probe onto the surface of the diamond, and the little light will give you the correct answer every time.

My recommendation: Cees Diamond Probe II from Gem Instruments, order #323000.

Gold Tester

Is it 10K, 14K, or 18K? An electronic gold tester knows for sure and gives you a fast and accurate reading of the purity of any piece of gold jewelry.

My recommendation: The G-XL-24-Pro® Portable Gold Tester, with a dynamic extended range of 6K to 24K and many features, is the best on the market, from Gem Instruments, order #102005.

Megascope

If someone asked me to write about the Universe at length, I could write a text with many volumes. The same would be true if I tried to write at length about the Megascope. Simply put, it is the greatest invention I've ever seen for measuring a diamond's proportions! It is 35 times more accurate than any human eye measurement (H.E.M.). It tells you the table percentage, crown angle, pavilion angle, total depth percentage, girdle thickness, diameter, length (if applicable), width (if applicable), and on and on. It tells you stuff you didn't think hard enough to ask! Quite frankly, if you are serious about making a career in diamonds, you must have a Megascope. Would you play basketball without a ball?

My recommendation: Megascope by OGI Systems LTD. (Point 2000).

All of the equipment listed is available from Point 2000, Gem Instruments, or Kassoy, three wonderful suppliers to the trade. Call them for the latest prices and to order merchandise.

Point 2000
580 5th Avenue, Ste. 2200
New York, NY 10036
(212) 768-2226
Orders, Toll-Free:
   (800) 223-5566

Gem Instruments
5355 Armada Drive, Ste. 300
Carlsbad, CA 92008
(780) 603-4200
Orders, Toll-Free:
(800) 421-8161

Kassoy
16 Midland Avenue
Hicksville, NY 11801
(800) 452-7769

INDEX

fractures, 93–94
defined, 87
Fred Connection, The, 102
"Fred's Complete Guide to
Sorting and Cleaning
Jewelry," 13, 229–232
Fred's Help Line, 103

G
Gem Instruments, 146, 233–234
gem microscope, 236
gem trade laboratories, 156–157
Gemological Institute of America
(GIA), and GIA-
certified, 14, 20–23, 61,
88, 125, 130–136, 141,
149–150, 156–160, 168
gemologists, 14
Getting Started checklist, 180
gift reminder/wish list, 104, 106,
109–112
girdle, 77, 142, 146–147
thickness, 150–151
gold dumping, 29
gold tester, 234
Gold/Platinum Dump Value
Table, 30–31
grading tips, 97

H
Help Line, 179
honest independent appraisers,
13, 15
Hope Diamond, 95
How to Buy a Diamond, xxii, 81,
86
hue, defined, 33
human eye measurement, 150

I
inclusions, xxiv, 23, 86–89, 90–94,
97
independent appraisers, 20
International Gem Institute (IGI),
61, 157–160

J
jeweler's denial mode, 7
jewelry store appraiser, 15

K
karats, defined, 20, 29

L
lab certificates, 61
length-to-width ratios, 148–149
leverage gauge, 76, 147, 233
liquidation value, 128
liquidity value, defined, xix
loupe, 17, 21, 22, 63, 86–87, 97,
233

M
mailing lists, 104–105
master set, 18, 95–96, 236
measuring a diamond's diameter,
143–144
media planners, 173–176
milky, defined 34

N
natural, defined 87
New York Diamond Dealers Club,
101–102, 112
newsletter, 104, 108
nicks, xxiii
non-Certified appraisers, 14